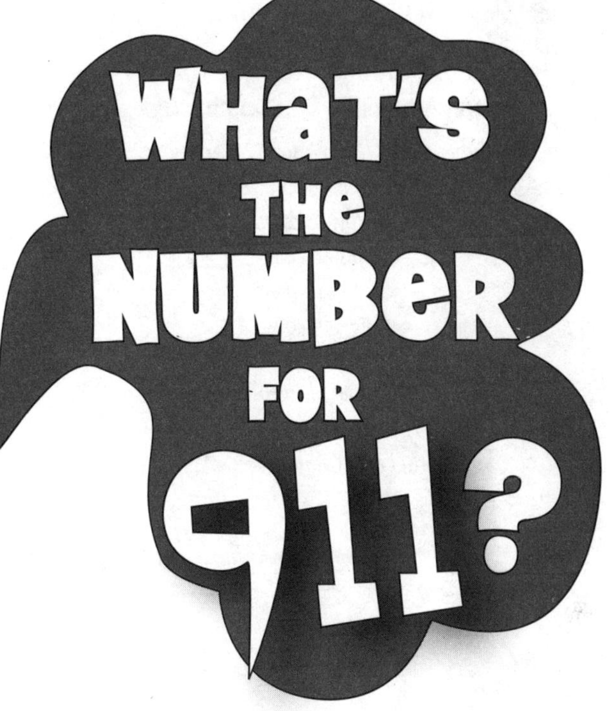
WHAT'S
THE
NUMBER
FOR
911?

OTHER BOOKS BY LELAND GREGORY

What's the Number for 911 Again?

The Stupid Crook Book

Hey, Idiot!

Idiots at Work

Bush-Whacked

Idiots in Love

Am-Bushed!

Stupid History

Idiots in Charge

Cruel and Unusual Idiots

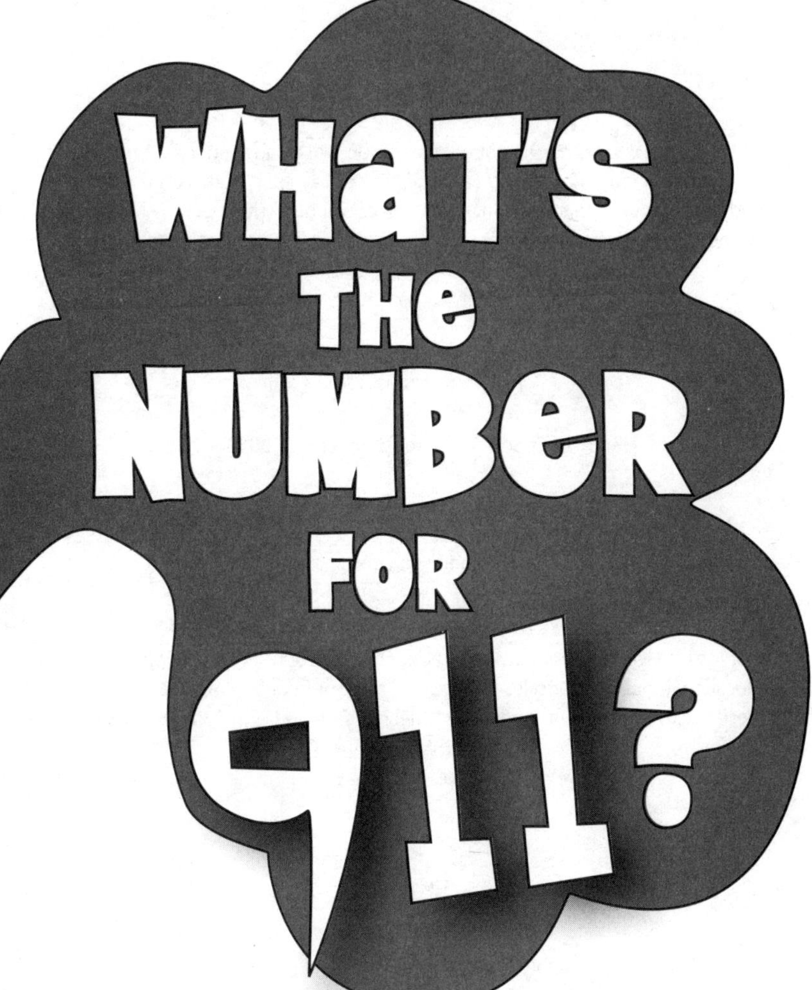

LELAND GREGORY

Andrews McMeel
Publishing, LLC

Kansas City

ISBN-13: 978-0-7407-7709-7
ISBN-10: 0-7407-7709-2

Library of Congress Control Number: 2008923007

08 09 10 11 12 MLT 10 9 8 7 6 5 4 3 2 1

www.andrewsmcmeel.com

This book is dedicated to my wife,
Gloria Graves Gregory,
who was the answer to my call for help
nearly twenty years ago.

Sickeningly Suite

DISPATCHER: 911. What is your emergency?

FEMALE CALLER: Yes, we just got to our hotel room and there are four of us here—but we only have enough towels for two.

DISPATCHER: This is 911, ma'am.

CALLER: Yes, well, what am I supposed to do?

DISPATCHER: Have you tried the hotel operator?

Long Live the King

DISPATCHER: 911. Fire or emergency?

CALLER: Oh, I would have to say emergency.

DISPATCHER: What's the problem, ma'am?

CALLER: There's a fight going on . . . it's . . . down there . . . I can see them through my window. They're in the parking lot. Oh, there's lots of yelling. They're cursing, too.

DISPATCHER: Can you describe who's fighting please?

CALLER: I'll try. There's one man and he's dressed like Elvis Presley. He's kicking another man who's laying on the ground and screaming "you ain't nothing but a hound dog."

Guilty before Proven Guilty

DISPATCHER: South Valley Dispatch.

BURGLAR: Yeah hi, um I just broke into a building, I'm inside the building right now, and I just got frustrated. I'm really upset right now—all I did was break the window and I walked away and I felt really guilty about it.

DISPATCHER: Do you know what the name of it is, or anything like that?

BURGLAR: I could go look really quick if you want to hold on a minute.

DISPATCHER: Okay will you come back?

BURGLAR: Yeah, I will.

DISPATCHER: Okay.

BURGLAR: Hold on a second. Now I'm gonna put the phone down.

DISPATCHER: All right, put your hand in the air and walk out there.

BURGLAR: Okay. I'm doing it right now.

DISPATCHER: Okay, good.

BURGLAR: Okay, bye.

DISPATCHER: Bye.

In and Outie

After a 911 call, paramedics were immediately dispatched to an "abdominal evisceration." They safely suited up in high-risk gloves, face shields, and other emergency gear. When they arrived at the residence, they found a thirteen-year-old boy lying motionless on the bed. They looked for a wound and examined the boy, but didn't find anything wrong. When they asked why he called 911, he said because he had "stuff" coming out of his navel. Further investigation revealed the "stuff" to be belly-button lint.

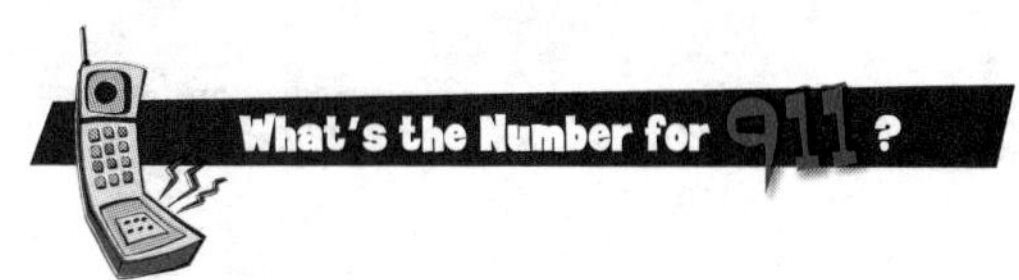

---911 Report---

Male complainant called and requested police call gas stations on all I-95 exits to find out which ones were open.

Stop Bugging Me

DISPATCHER: Allegheny 911.

CALLER: I have a praying mantis in my bedroom. My friend told me I would go to jail if I touch it.

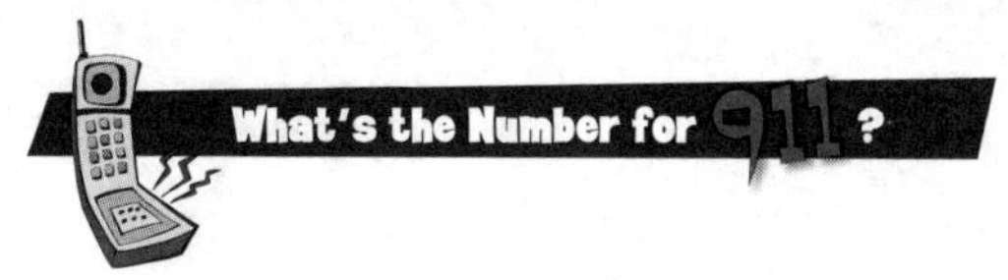

I Smell a Rat

DISPATCHER: 911. What is your emergency?

TERRIFIED FEMALE CALLER: Yes, I'd like to report a wild animal in my house.

DISPATCHER: Yes.

CALLER: It's wild. It's a mouse.

DISPATCHER: I'm sorry, ma'am, you said it was a mouse?

CALLER: Yes! Yes! That's what I said. A mouse.

Pillow Talk

"I was expecting the worst," said police communications unit director Frieda Lehner about a suicide call she received several years ago. The depressed man called the Albuquerque police headquarters, and Lehner engaged him in a conversation trying to talk the man out of any rash moves. They discussed his divorce and custody battle, about his tour in Vietnam, and how he finally wound up living with his mother because he was unable to get a job even though he tried. Lehner recalled that the man grew more and more agitated about how rotten his life had become. Suddenly, and to her horror, she heard a gunshot over the phone line. Then Lehner heard the phone drop—and then there was silence.

Soon she could hear the rustling of the phone being picked back up. "He came back on the line and he was extremely upset. He was using some very good adjectives. I was saying, 'Are you hurt?' He said, 'I just shot my mother's favorite pillow. She's going to kill me.' That one was very stressful, but it turned out real good."

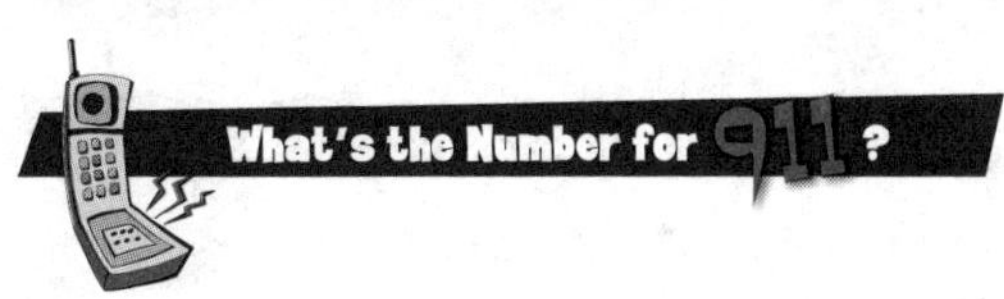

---911 Report---

"My parrot got out and is in a tree outside."

Teenage Wasteland

DISPATCHER: 911, what is your emergency?

WOMAN: Yes, I need a police officer over here at ____________.

DISPATCHER: What's going on?

WOMAN: I've got two teenage daughters and I just got home from work. They were physically fighting with each other and one of them kicked a hole in a door and they're twelve and almost fourteen and uh, the twelve-year-old is completely out of control and I can't physically . . . she's as big as I am. I can't control her.

DISPATCHER: Okay, did you want us to come over and shoot her?

[long pause]

DISPATCHER: Are you there?

WOMAN: Excuse me?

DISPATCHER: That's a joke. Okay . . .

WOMAN: Who are you? What is your name?

DISPATCHER: Mike _______.

WOMAN: Okay, that's not funny, Mike.

DISPATCHER: I know it's not, ma'am. I apologize . . .

WOMAN: Well, guess what? It's not going to be very funny when I go in front of your supervisor and tell him . . .

DISPATCHER: I'm sorry. I apologize.

WOMAN: Well, sorry doesn't cut it.

DISPATCHER: Okay. All right. I'll get police officers on the way. They're on an emergency call right now but as soon as I can get one free I'll get them on the way.

WOMAN: [sarcastically] Well, don't rush or anything.

DISPATCHER: Well, I, I apologize for my smart remark and I will get a man out as soon as I can.

Check, Please

DISPATCHER: 911, what's your emergency?

MAN: Well, let me tell you. My girlfriend, Sue, and I have been together for about three years now, see?

DISPATCHER: Sir, do you have an emergency?

MAN: Here's the thing. Why I called, see. I was hoping, you know, well, it's like, if you could send a cop by to see if she's home. And while they're there see what cars are parked in her driveway—and maybe write down their license numbers and stuff. Since you guys can do stuff like that—you can find out who the cars belong too, right? Find out if she's there and who's there with her and stuff. I think she's cheating on me but I don't have no proof . . . so, could you do that, you think?

DISPATCHER: Sir, this number is for emergency calls only. I'm sorry, but we can't help you.

MAN: Sh—t!

Boy, That Sucked!

At 4:45 a.m., a clerk at the Scottish Inn Motel called the Lakeland, Florida, 911 emergency and reported that a man was stuck in the swimming pool. When police and paramedics arrived, they quickly discovered the problem. A man's penis was caught in the suction fitting of the motel's swimming pool. "As I approached the man," went an officer's report, "I could see his pants were down to his knees and his penis was stuck in a suction hole located in the north-side wall of the swimming pool."

Although the pool's pump had been shut off before the police arrived, the man's penis had swollen so much that he couldn't remove it from the suction hole. Paramedics lubricated the fitting and were finally able to "free willy" after about forty minutes. I'll bet the man was so sore after his little mishap he won't be doing the backstroke for a long time.

---911 Report---

"I've got a roach stuck in my ear."

a Phone Bug

DISPATCHER: Sheriff's Department.

MALE CALLER: Yeah, I have an ant in my ear, and I tried to flush it out with water, but that only made it go in further . . . What should I do? It's buggin' the hell out of my eardrum.

Not Schooled in 911 Etiquette

Early one morning, a four-year-old made an emergency call to police in Essen, Germany. The little boy begged the officer for help: He didn't want to go to kindergarten. After the child hung up, police called back and spoke to the boy's mother. She said her son had threatened to call the police if she made him go—but she didn't believe him. The story doesn't end on a happy note: The boy ended up going to kindergarten after all.

a Real Dope

DISPATCHER: Sheriff's Department.

MALE CALLER: Yeah, do you deliver dope? . . . Ahh, me and my girlfriend, we need some dope.

DISPATCHER: Sir, this is the Sheriff's Department.

[Click.]

DISPATCHER: Hello. Hello.

Man Overboard

An inebriated, fifty-two-year-old man in Copenhagen, Denmark, who was playing with toy boats in his bathtub, phoned in several "mayday" calls to an emergency center claiming his ship was going down in the Baltic Sea.

911 REPORT

Man called and requested dispatcher call his wife to let her know he's on his way home and that she shouldn't yell at him.

---911 Report---

A Dorsey Drive convalescent facility reported that one Alzheimer's patient struck another Alzheimer's patient, but neither of them remembered the incident or wanted medical attention.

a Shooting Pain

Gail Murphy fired a shotgun through the front door of her house and then dialed 911. It seems that Gail, who was recovering from hemorrhoid surgery, was furious when her husband, Edward, went fishing with his buddies rather than stay home with her. Although she was forced to remain in bed on her stomach after the surgery, Gail could still aim the shotgun at the door. So, when her husband returned home six hours later, she shot him. Seems like he had been a pain in her rear longer than the hemorrhoids. Edward died of his wounds a few days later.

911 REPORT

When is the Cinco de Mayo [Fifth of May] celebration?

---911 Report---

Female complainant called to request police officer come to residence to change battery in smoke detector as she couldn't reach it.

Hold the anchovies

DISPATCHER: 911. What is your emergency?

MALE CALLER: Yeah, I want to order a pizza.

DISPATCHER: You need to call 411.

a Rose by any Other Name

DISPATCHER: 911. Please state the nature of your emergency.

CALLER: I just thought you'd like to know that someone has trespassed on my property.

DISPATCHER: Okay, ma'am. Was anything damaged or taken?

CALLER: That's why I called. Someone trimmed my rosebushes. Now, I'm the only one who trims my bushes and I would know when they'd been trimmed. I just thought you'd like to know—I think my next-door neighbor did it. She's a mean old bitch.

911? High, How are You?

After the 911 center in Sioux Falls, South Dakota, received an emergency hang-up call, they dispatched a patrol car to make certain that the female caller was all right. When police arrived the woman said she called 911 because a male acquaintance had taken her marijuana. But, she assured them, everything was fine now because he had returned it. Police, however, informed her that things weren't okay and seized her pot, arrested her, and took her to jail. The woman pleaded guilty to drug possession and was fined one hundred dollars. Lt. Mark Moberly reported that she didn't seem stoned when she called 911. "Some people are just kind of naturally high," he added. "Especially out here where the air is so clear."

911 REPORT

What's the phone number for police?

911 One-Liners

911 Report:
"Please connect me to Switzerland."

911 Report:
"I have the hiccups."

911 Report:
"My neighbor's dog is barking."

911 Report:
"When is my power coming back on?"

911 Report:
"A thirteen-year-old stubbed her toe on a stereo speaker."

911 Report:
"I'd like to make a unanimous complaint, so don't use my name."

911 Report:
Male complainant called to report a squirrel on his front porch.

Dying for Attention

A man called 911 and told the operator he was having suicidal thoughts and needed help. Police, paramedics, and firefighters were on the scene in minutes. They were surprised and annoyed when the man told them that he never really wanted to kill himself, and it was only a joke—but since they were there, and he was drunk, could they give him a ride uptown.

---911 Report---

"My nail is broken."

a Pain in the Neck

DISPATCHER: This is the ambulance emergency line. Do you have an emergency?

MAN: I need an ambulance.

DISPATCHER: Who is this?

MAN: Uh, Joe.

DISPATCHER: Okay, Joe. Where do you need us?

MAN: I'm in the m— f—ing phone booth.

DISPATCHER: Okay, what's the address there?

MAN: Uh, I'm in the m— f—ing phone booth at the Stop & Go. Let me tell you what. I'm at the . . .I'm going down the m— f—ing road driving in my car minding my own g— d— business and a m— f—ing deer jumps out and hits my car.

DISPATCHER: Okay, sir. Are you injured?

MAN: Let . . . now, let me tell you. I get out and pick the m— f—ing deer up. I thought he was dead. I put the m— f—ing deer in my backseat and I'm driving down the m— f—ing road and minding my own business. The m— f—er woke

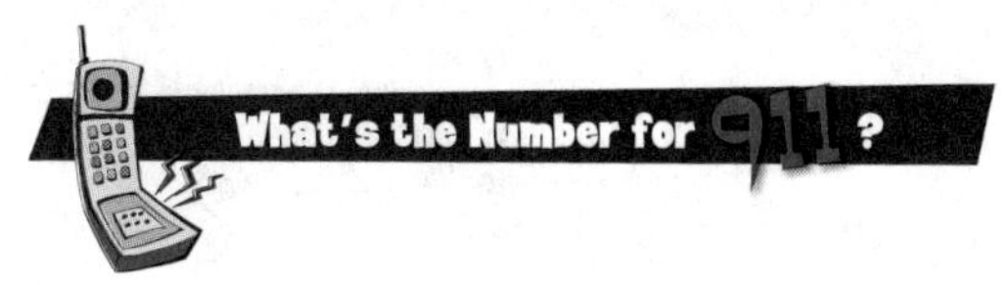

up and bit me in the back of my g— d— neck and he bit me and he done kicked the sh— out of my car. I'm in the m— f—ing phone booth. The deer bit me in the neck. A big m— f—ing dog came up and bit me in the leg and I hit him with the m— f—ing tire iron and I stabbed him, I stabbed him with my knife. So, I got a hurt leg and the m— f—ing deer bit me in the neck. And the deer . . . the dog won't let me out of the m— f—ing phone booth, 'cause he wants the deer. Now, who gets the deer, me or the dog?

DISPATCHER: Okay, sir. Are you injured?

MAN: Yeah, m— f—ing deer bit me in the neck. Hold on. Let . . .hey, the m— f—ing dog is biting me! Hold on! The m— f—ing dog is biting me. Hold on! g— d—it, get out of here. Hold on! The m— f—ing dog is biting my ass. Hold on!

Car alarm

DISPATCHER: 911.

FRANTIC WOMAN: I have a crisis and I'm having a breakdown. Oh, my God!!!

DISPATCHER: Somebody injured?

FRANTIC WOMAN: No, no! My life is about to be messed up! Oh, my God, can somebody please come and help me?

DISPATCHER: What, what's going on?

FRANTIC WOMAN: My license has expired, and I'm being told that there is nothing that anyone can do to help me! I need a—I need a license! I need help!

DISPATCHER: You're at the DMV, right?

FRANTIC WOMAN: Yes!

DISPATCHER: Ma'am?

FRANTIC WOMAN: Yes?

DISPATCHER: You need to calm down, okay?

FRANTIC WOMAN: Oh, my God!

Well, Bite Me, Too!

A mother of a three-year-old called 911 at midnight claiming her child was having a severe allergic reaction to an insect bite. Paramedics arrived minutes later and found the child breathing normally with no apparent signs of an allergic reaction—no swelling, no rash. The mother told them her daughter had been bitten by a mosquito. However, when the paramedics examined the little girl all they found were light scratch marks that hadn't even scraped the skin. The mother then explained that the mosquito had bitten her daughter about four days ago. Waiting that long was a stupid mistake—now they'll never be able to track down the mosquito for questioning.

---911 Report---

Male complainant called because he didn't want to bother looking up the sheriff's office phone number in the phone book.

a Grainy Image

DISPATCHER: 911.

CALLER: Yes, I need to report an emergency.

DISPATCHER: Is this at Garvey Grain? Where at, sir?

CALLER: I live at, uh, the . . . on Fourth Street.

DISPATCHER: OK, what happened?

CALLER: It felt like something ran into my house. I come outside and there's a great big cloud of smoke just southwest.

DISPATCHER: OK, we just got a report that Garvey Grain just blew up, would that be it?

CALLER: That's probably what it is.

---911 Report---

"What were the winning numbers for the evening Pick Four today?"

From Stand-Up to Lockdown

A forty-four-year-old man from Richburg, South Carolina, pulled a practical joke on his wife. He splattered ketchup all over himself, fired a shot from his .22-caliber rifle into the air, and then lay down on the floor as if dead. When his wife heard the shot, she ran into the next room. As soon as she saw her husband's lifeless body she became frantic and called 911. Deputies were not amused by the man's joke, but they did have the last laugh. Apparently, the prankster forgot that he had a criminal record, making it a felony for him to possess a firearm. He was arrested and eventually sentenced to fifteen years to life in prison. So, the joke was on him.

---911 Report---

"My dog is choking or having a seizure. What do I do?"

If the Truth Be Known

DISPATCHER: 911. Fire or emergency?

CALLER: Neither. My son was bothering me. I just wanted to let you know.

Room with a View

DISPATCHER: 911, what's the nature of your emergency?

WOMAN: [whispering] Is this 911?

DISPATCHER: Yes, ma'am, it is.

WOMAN: [whispering] Oh, good. I'm glad I finally got someone who can help me.

DISPATCHER: Are you in trouble, ma'am?

WOMAN: [whispering] Oh, yes, yes—a lot of trouble, I believe.

DISPATCHER: Is someone in the room with you?

WOMAN: [whispering] No. I don't see anyone.

DISPATCHER: Then why are you whispering? What's your emergency?

WOMAN: I'm a hospital patient, and I think an orderly wants to see me naked.

Someone's Been Sleeping in My Bed

A twenty-six-year-old man called a Madison, Wisconsin, emergency center, and reported that an intruder was in his home. The man explained that when he returned from the bathroom in the middle of the night, he saw a stranger, wearing only boxer shorts, sleeping in his bed. Although skeptical of the call, the 911 operator followed regulations and dispatched an officer to the residence—and yes, there was someone sleeping in this man's bed, and it wasn't Goldilocks. The drunken stranger was a twenty-two-year-old college student from DePere, Wisconsin. Hum . . . an intoxicated college student—never heard of one of those before.

---911 Report---

Complainant says unknown male has been living in her house. Complainant is partially blind and just found his clothing.

Map Quest

DISPATCHER: What location are you calling from?

CALLER: I'm not calling from a location. I'm calling from my cell phone.

Break Like the Wind

Police in Janesville, Wisconsin, responded to a 911 domestic disturbance call. When they arrived at the location, the wife claimed the argument started when she and her husband were tucking their son into bed—and he inappropriately passed gas.

911 REPORT

"Just wanted to check and see if it was really working."

Bosom Buddies, Lifelong Pals

DISPATCHER: 911. Fire or emergency?

CALLER: Um, [cough] emergency, I guess.

DISPATCHER: What's the nature of your emergency, sir?

CALLER: [cough] You see, my friend, Jack, we've been drinking, you see, and suddenly he just falls over on the floor there.

DISPATCHER: How much have you had to drink?

CALLER: Not enough for that to happen, man. [cough] We've been more drunk than this before—lots of times. This is a first. He don't look so good, you probably ought to send someone around real soon.

DISPATCHER: Is he breathing?

CALLER: I'll check. [*Puts phone down. Pause. He gets back on the line.*] I don't think so—not like he normally breathes, you know. He don't look too good.

DISPATCHER: Do you want to do CPR till the paramedics arrive?

CALLER: I can't do that. I still have a bad cold.

Trophy Bride

DISPATCHER: 911, what's your emergency?

CALLER: It's my old lady, she's gone crazy!

DISPATCHER: What's the problem, sir?

CALLER: She's tearing through the house, throwing sh—t around. Broke out a g— d— window with my f—ing bowling trophy. She said she's going to kill me, man. F—ing hell, I believe her too!

DISPATCHER: Does she have any weapons?

CALLER: Well, she has real long fingernails.

Nearly Hog Heaven

Tracy Mosier, a 911 dispatcher from Kelso, Washington, was trained in giving instructions on the Heimlich maneuver. So she was ready when this call came in. Well, maybe, she was ready. "My pig! She choked and she passed out." Mosier was happy to help and calmly coached the frantic caller step-by-step until the pig was revived. She said that she's also proficient in giving mouth-to-snout resuscitation.

---911 Report---

"Can you tell me when the next earthquake is?"

Or Was It a Potpie?

DISPATCHER: Emergency.

MAN: Yeah, can you please send rescue? I think I'm having an overdose and so is my wife.

DISPATCHER: Overdose of what?

MAN: Marijuana. I don't know if it had something in it.

DISPATCHER: Oh, okay. How old are you?

MAN: I'm twenty-eight, uh, twenty-nine-years-old and my wife is uh, twenty-six—please come.

DISPATCHER: Have you guys been drinking, also?

MAN: What?

DISPATCHER: Have you guys been drinking today, too?

MAN: No, that's it. Please come.

DISPATCHER: Do you have a fever or anything?

MAN: No, I just, I think we're dying.

DISPATCHER: How much did you guys have?

MAN: I don't know, we made brownies and I think we're dead. I really do.

DISPATCHER: How much did you put in the brownies? Was it a bag?

MAN: I don't know. Time is going by really, really, really, really slow.

DISPATCHER: Was it a big batch? A little batch?

MAN: It was a quarter ounce.

DISPATCHER: Okay, but brownie-wise, how many pieces do you guys think you guys had?

MAN: I don't know. I probably had like a small chunk. Please come.

DISPATCHER: Do you guys do this on a regular basis?

MAN: No, this is the first time that we've ever done it.

[later in the phone call]

MAN: What's the score on the Red Wings game?

DISPATCHER: What?

MAN: What's the score on the Red Wings game?

DISPATCHER: I've got no clue. I don't watch the Red Wings.

MAN: Okay, I just want to make sure this isn't some type of hallucination I'm having.

DISPATCHER: Why? What does the score say?

MAN: Three to three.

DISPATCHER: What channel is it on?

MAN: Uh . . . channel 2.

DISPATCHER: Mmmmmm . . . it's two to two.

MAN: Okay, your police, tell your officers they just passed me.

DISPATCHER: Oh, we'll let them know, okay. Go outside and flag them down, okay?

MAN: Okay. Um, my mother-in-law just got here, too.

DISPATCHER: All righty. Bye.

Don't Cry over Spilled Beer

After a hang-up call at the 911 dispatch center in Des Moines, Iowa, police were immediately dispatched to the residence. They then learned that the caller had inadvertently dialed 911 while wiping spilled beer off his phone. When police ran a routine check, they discovered that the caller had an outstanding warrant for his arrest on drug possession and failure to appear in court. His day now went from "It's Miller Time" to "It's Prison Time."

---911 Report---

"These bee droppings are ruining my roof!"

Deep Throat Returns

DISPATCHER: 911. Fire or emergency?

MAN: I know what you're up to.

DISPATCHER: Excuse me, sir?

MAN: I can't excuse you. I know what you've been doing and who you are and don't think I don't know.

DISPATCHER: I'm sorry, sir. Do you have an emergency to report?

MAN: I'm going to report each of you to the CIA—you'll go to jail for what you've been doing.

DISPATCHER: I'm sorry, sir. I don't understand what you're talking about.

MAN: Sure you don't. I've got the number of the Secret Service and they're already on to you guys. Don't say I didn't warn you!

an alarmist

Operators at the Gainesville, Florida, 911 center dispatched sheriff's deputies after receiving a call to respond to a car alarm and to check on the caller's statement that there was a man locked inside the car trying to kick out a window. When they arrived, deputies found a fifty-one-year-old man, "trying to hide, all scrunched down in the back seat." The thief thought he was trapped because the alarm system had automatically locked the car doors when it was tripped. "I guess he thought deputies couldn't see him. Had he pushed the button on the driver's side door, he could have gotten out." Getting out of the next place into which he was locked wouldn't be so easy.

---911 Report---

"Yeah, my cable's out. Can you send someone around?"

Pound Foolish

DISPATCHER (ENGLAND): 999.

MAN: I was upstairs shopping in Iceland's [supermarket]. I put a pound in one of them trolleys [shopping cart] because you know you've got to get the pound in the trolley . . .

DISPATCHER: Can you tell me exactly what your emergency is—you just dialed 999.

MAN: When the trolley comes back I'm supposed to get a pound back.

DISPATCHER: That's enough. I'm not taking this call on the emergency line. The fact that you didn't get your pound back out of the trolley isn't an emergency situation.

One Word—Sounds Like . . .

DISPATCHER: 911. What's your emergency?

CALLER: Uh, my grandfather just died. Can you send someone around here to pick him up?

DISPATCHER: You say your grandfather died?

CALLER: Yeah, a few minutes ago, I guess. He was real old and he's been sick a while. He finally just died.

DISPATCHER: Could you give me your address, please?

CALLER: Sure. It's the Fall Vista apartments on Thurgood. Apartment 34D.

DISPATCHER: Apartment 34?

CALLER: D, D, as in dead.

---911 Report---

"There's a rat in my house. Could you please send someone over to kill it?"

Crap Out of Luck

Neighbors have feuded with one another since the dawn of man. However, one set of nasty neighbors had been at real odds with each other for years. One finally got so disgusted at what the other had done that he called 911 to complain. Evidently, the neighbor had trained his dog to go out of his own yard and poop on a rock near the man's mailbox.

Date Line

DISPATCHER: 911. Do you need fire, medical, or police?

WOMAN: No, ma'am, I don't. I don't have an emergency. Two police officers just left my house just now. Can I get their names, please?

DISPATCHER: What was the problem?

WOMAN: Nothing. He was just the cutest cop I've seen in God knows how long. I just wanted his name. I'm sorry, I know it's not an emergency. But it's not very often that a good-looking man comes up to your doorstep. [pause] Could you send him back my way?

DISPATCHER: You need him to come back there?

WOMAN: Oh, I'd like that, yeah!

DISPATCHER: Why do you need him to come back there?

WOMAN: Because I have an emergency. I'll think of something.

DISPATCHER: Ma'am . . .

WOMAN: Honey, I'm just going to be honest with you, okay? I just thought he was cute. I'm forty-five-years-old and I'd just like to meet him again, but I don't know how to go about doing that without calling 911.

Nuts for Knots

Police in Houma, Louisiana, issued a citation to a woman for improper use of the 911 emergency line because she called 911 to report the following "emergency situation": her husband was preventing her from watching the season finale of *Knots Landing*.

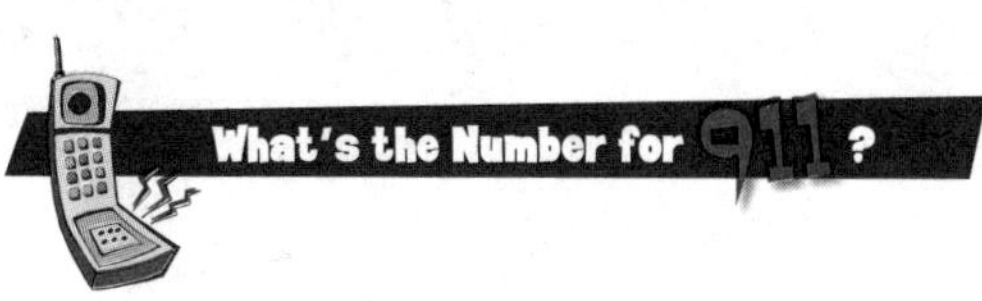

---911 Report---

"Would you send the fire department to our address? We need them to get our pet parakeet out of a tree."

No, You're a Real Meatball

DISPATCHER: 911, is this an emergency?

WOMAN: Could you tell me how to make meatballs?

DISPATCHER: Could I tell you how to make meatballs?

WOMAN: Yes.

DISPATCHER: Ma'am, this is 911 emergency services.

WOMAN: This is an emergency.

DISPATCHER: Ma'am, I cannot tell you that.

WOMAN: Okay, thank you.

DISPATCHER: Good-bye.

Must Be the New

DISPATCHER: 911, what's the nature of your emergency, please?

WOMAN: I'm trying to reach nine-eleven, but my phone doesn't have an eleven on it.

DISPATCHER: This is 9-11.

WOMAN: I thought you just said it was nine-one-one.

DISPATCHER: Yes, ma'am, nine-one-one and nine-eleven are the same thing.

WOMAN: Honey, I may be old but I'm not stupid!

If the Car's a Rockin' . . .

In Vancouver, two city police cars, who were responding to a 911 emergency call about a stolen vehicle, accidentally crashed head-on. Fortunately the officers weren't badly hurt. It seems the emergency wasn't about a stolen sedan but about a cuddling codger. This unusual event started when a man called 911 to report that his father's car was being stolen, however, there weren't any thieves—just the seventy-two-year-old owner of the car and a female prostitute. It turns out the son was upset because his father was routinely hiring prostitutes, so he called 911 hoping it would deter his father's activity. And they say an old dog can't turn new tricks.

---911 Report---

"Uh, I need some help. Seems I locked my keys in the car again."

Padded Room with a View

DISPATCHER: Police, fire, and medical.

WOMAN: I have never been in Portland before except once to pick up a check and I don't know where to go. I'm near an adult bookstore called Cindy's . . .

DISPATCHER: Okay, do you need police, fire, or medical?

WOMAN: No sir, I want to know where a good place to sit quietly and be by myself is.

DISPATCHER: Let me transfer you to nonemergency. I think they have a place for you.

Driven to Extremes

DISPATCHER: 911. Fire or emergency?

CALLER: This is Ed Dodsworth at 705 Elm Street. I put an ad in the paper to sell my 1992 Dodge Dart and some guy wanted a test drive. That was three hours ago and he hasn't come back.

DISPATCHER: We'll need a description of him.

CALLER: He's a lawyer.

Food for Thought

An angry man called the British emergency number, 999, and demanded help from the Avon and Somerset police. "My wife's left me with two salmon sandwiches which was left over from last night, and I'm sat in the chair here and she's out there decorating," the man told the operator. "She won't put any food on or anything for anybody." The operator interrupted the man's tirade, "I'm sorry but I really can't take this. It's not an emergency because your wife won't give you anything to eat." I'm sure all emergency operators get their fill of calls like this.

---911 Report---

Female called to report she needed to go to the toilet.

Don't Be Such a Pussy!

DISPATCHER: 911, fire or emergency?

MAN: Not sure. A cat just walked into the house I'm in and gave birth to kittens!

DISPATCHER: Sir, this is 911.

MAN: What do I do? Should I wash them? They look like they need to be washed.

DISPATCHER: Just let nature take its course, sir. I'm sure the cat will be able to take care of the kittens just fine without any assistance.

Lock and Load

DISPATCHER: 911, where is your emergency?

WOMAN: I'm out here riding around and I locked my keys in the car. Is there anyway someone could come out here and unlock my car?

DISPATCHER: Uh, commercial services are available in town to do that, ma'am—police and fire cannot.

WOMAN: What do you mean, "commercial services"?

DISPATCHER: I mean, you'll have to pay to have it done.

Cover Your Head

Police officers were immediately dispatched when an elderly woman called 911 to report that there was an animal in her closet. Once on the scene, a tall, strong officer confidently marched over to the closet door, opened it, and looked around. Suddenly, he slammed the door and called headquarters requesting that Animal Control be sent over at once. As soon as they arrived, they quickly spotted the furry fiend: It was a fur hat that had fallen from a hook. Since the officer who had requested Animal Control was already on another call, the dispatcher decided to put the word out on the radio. Now, every police officer on duty who had their radio on heard the following: "Animal Control confirms the capture of a hat, I repeat a hat. H.A.T. Not a Bat or a Cat but a Hat. It is now confined to a hatbox in the closet and will not do any more attacking tonight."

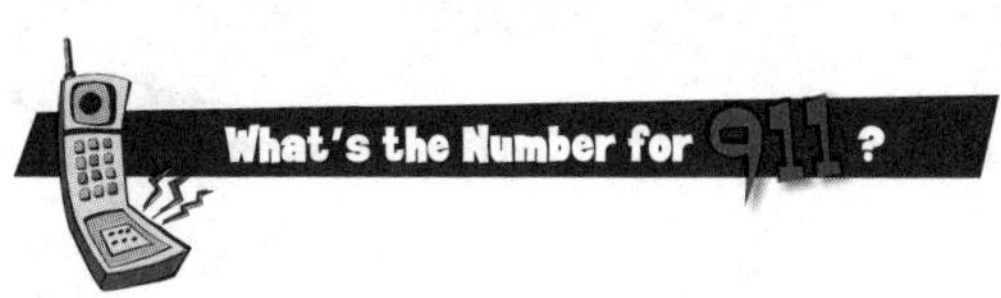

---911 Report---

"There's a rat in my kitchen."

Unclear Reception

DISPATCHER: 911, what's your emergency?

CALLER: I want to report a consumer fraud, please.

DISPATCHER: Ma'am, 911 is for emergencies only.

CALLER: Well, I don't know who else to call. My television set doesn't work. The man I bought it from won't give me my money back.

Well, It Rhymes with Truck

A twenty-year-old man from Verona, Kentucky, called 911 and insisted that someone had "thrown" his truck on top of him. But, after being questioned, the caller admitted he was drunk, had been involved in a single-vehicle accident, and was trapped upside-down in his truck. Although he was in excruciating pain, he stayed on the line for more than two hours refusing to disclose his location. But, as the *Kentucky Enquirer* put it, "When repeatedly asked his location, the answer was always the same: 'I'm under the (expletive) truck.'" Eventually, he gave the operator a clue to his location and was rescued.

Call Me an Ambulance. Okay, You're an Ambulance!

DISPATCHER: 911, what's your emergency?

WOMAN: There's a lady on the ground here in the emergency room and they are overlooking her.

DISPATCHER: What would you want me to do for you, ma'am?

WOMAN: Send an ambulance out here to pick her up and take her somewhere where she can get medical help.

DISPATCHER: Okay, you're at the hospital, ma'am. You would have to contact them.

WOMAN: They are the problem—they won't help her. Down, all down on the ground.

DISPATCHER: Well, ma'am, I cannot do anything for you for the quality of the hospital there. This line is for emergency purposes only.

WOMAN: This is an emergency, mister.

DISPATCHER: It's not an emergency.

WOMAN: It is.

DISPATCHER: It is not an emergency, ma'am.

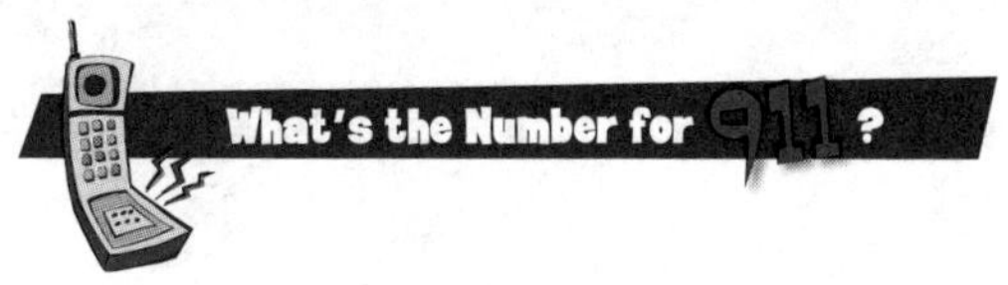

WOMAN: It is.

DISPATCHER: It's not an emergency.

WOMAN: Come down here and see how they are treating her.

DISPATCHER: Well, okay, that's not a criminal thing. This line, 911, is used for emergency purposes only.

WOMAN: This is an emergency.

DISPATCHER: It is not.

WOMAN: May God strike you, too! For acting the way you did.

I Thought It Was a Very Small Bandit!!!

DISPATCHER: 911, where is your emergency?

WOMAN: Uh, 608 Court.

DISPATCHER: What's going on there?

WOMAN: Uh, there's some raccoons in my attic. Uh, they made their way into the attic somehow from outside.

DISPATCHER: Okay, you dialed 911 for raccoons in your attic?

WOMAN: Well, yeah, because Animal Control came out one other time. I haven't called my landlord 'cause I ran—I didn't know if I should call her first.

DISPATCHER: Well, you definitely need to call your landlord. But next time you need to call on the administrative line—this is taking up an emergency line.

I'll Give Your Hide a Good Tanning

Police and firefighters thought it might be their lucky day when they were dispatched to a residence where the female occupant was stuck in a tanning bed. However, when they arrived at the house in Norton Shores, Michigan, they found a naked sixty-year-old woman who had "gotten quite a tan." She had originally purchased the tanning machine to treat a skin condition, but the first time she tried it out, she accidentally slipped, the lid got stuck, and she couldn't turn it off. Luckily—although a little strange—the woman had taken her cordless phone into the tanning bed with her, and she used it to call 911. Police and firefighters immediately unplugged the machine, and then helped her out. While the scorched senior citizen stood before police and firefighters, they couldn't tell if she was red from embarrassment or just "well done."

---911 Report---

"Is it all right in Boulder to ask a woman for sex?"

a Birdbrained Call

DISPATCHER: 911.

WOMAN: Uh, hi, last night I put my turkey in . . .

DISPATCHER: Uh, huh?

WOMAN: . . . in the oven, and I set the, uh, oven at about two . . . twelve is what I was thinking, it's about a . . . twenty pound turkey. Is that safe?

DISPATCHER: Yeah, we really don't provide that kind of service, but I'm trying to help you out anyway. If it were me, I'd probably turn up the oven and just cook it and eat it.

WOMAN: Okay, thank you.

DISPATCHER: Yeah. Okay, good luck to you. Bye-bye.

The Wrong Pickup Line

A man from Candor, New York, was arrested after making a fake emergency call. Evidently he had a fetish for policewomen and called hoping they would send a "hot-looking" female officer.

911 REPORT

"Yeah, the battery in my cell phone is dead."

Take a Deep Breath

DISPATCHER: 911. Fire or emergency?

CALLER: Emergency. I need you to . . . I need an ambulance. Quick! Send one now!

DISPATCHER: What's the emergency, sir?

CALLER: It's my uncle. He's unconscious and I can't get him to wake up. Get an ambulance down here now. The address is 68 North Hampton. Hurry up!

DISPATCHER: Settle down, sir, and try to remain calm. An ambulance is on the way. Is your uncle breathing?

CALLER: He's not breathing!

DISPATCHER: Can you get the phone close to him?

CALLER: WHY? You want to hear he's not breathing, too?

911 Notes

A Vancouver police officer was sent to a home in the 3100 block of S Street . . . when a woman called 911 to say a group of 30 cannibals from Yacolt were trying to break into her house. Officers were unable to locate any cannibals.

Stupid in Thirty Minutes or Less

DISPATCHER: Arlington 911.

WOMAN: I'd like to be connected to Domino's Pizza please, in Arlington.

DISPATCHER: That's not a, this is 911, 911 is for police and fire emergencies.

WOMAN: Well I can't get through on the Pizza Hut line or 411.

DISPATCHER: Okay, well, ma'am, 911 does not connect you to Domino's Pizza.

Fast Food—Slow Witted

Police in Avon, Ohio, chose not to charge a woman for abusing the 911 system—even though she was guilty. She had called the emergency number to complain that a McDonald's restaurant tried to charge her for extra barbecue sauce. I guess they decided that eating at McDonald's was punishment enough.

---911 Report---

Woman called three times to report UFOs are coming to mechanize her brain.

Close the Trunk

DISPATCHER: Police communications, Elliot.

MAN: Hey, um, we found an elephant walking down the street near the community center, the Ray Twiney.

DISPATCHER: Sorry?

MAN: We found an elephant walking down the street. [pause] Like the ones from the circus at the Ray Twiney Center. One of them got loose and it's walking down the street.

DISPATCHER: What road is it walking down?

MAN: [to other person] What's the street? What's the street? Alex Stoner, I think. Alex Stoner near the exit of 320.

DISPATCHER: It's on Alex Stoner?

MAN: Yeah.

DISPATCHER: How big are we talking here?

MAN: [laughs] Like, full-grown elephant. It's like the ones they have at like the circus—that, like, the people ride on and stuff.

DISPATCHER: Right.

MAN: Yeah.

[People laughing in background]

DISPATCHER: Is there anyone around it at all?

MAN: Yeah. Yeah. [to someone else] I told him that, dear.

DISPATCHER: Is there anybody there like any sort of . . .?

MAN: No, no, it's just an elephant.

OTHER VOICE: It's following him, he's leading. . .

MAN: One of my friends, is like, it's following him and he's leading it right back there but . . .

DISPATCHER: Currently walking down Alex Stoner?

MAN: Yes.

DISPATCHER: What direction is it going in?

MAN: It's heading back toward the Ray . . .there's another one out, too.

OTHER VOICE: They're all out.

MAN: I think all three of the . . .

DISPATCHER: How many do you see?

MAN: We see two. We don't know if there's a third.

OTHER VOICE: Should we check this one? This one's right on my street. I don't want to go by it.

MAN: There's like, yeah, there's like two or three elephants out here. They're huge.

DISPATCHER: Well, we'll see what we can do here.

His Bark Is Worse Than His Bite

It was a Norman Rockwell Christmas. The stockings were hung by the chimney with care, the tree was decorated—and the dog was about to vomit on the carpet. When ten-year-old John saw his dog Pookie about to puke, he pushed the dog off the rug, inadvertently toppling the family's large artificial Christmas tree. After he pushed the tree back into its stand and checked on his dog the tree fell again—this time pinning the child under it. John couldn't get up, but he was able to reach a cordless phone. He called several people in his Fremont, Nebraska, neighborhood, but most weren't home and one "didn't believe me," said John. Finally, he dialed 911 and explained what had happened. Police and firefighters soon freed the young boy who wasn't hurt by the "Banzai" tree.

---911 Report---

"Where the hell are my food stamps?
I'm a taxpayer, you know!"

One from the "Duh" Files

DISPATCHER: Allegheny 911.

CALLER: When is the Fourth of July Parade?

The Blame Game

DISPATCHER: Akron 911. What is your emergency?

MAN: My old lady's going nuts. I don't want the blame for it. She's drunk. She bolted out the door. No shoes. No coat. I don't want the blame.

Ear-itating Neighbor

DISPATCHER: Akron 911. What's your emergency?

CALLER: There's this woman, you know? She lives in my neighborhood, she sticks something sharp in my ear. Will you tell her to stop it?

Up in Smoke

"I made some stupid mistakes," admitted a thirty-year-old Maryland man to the judge at his sentencing. Several months earlier, he had called 911 to report a fire on his property. "You gotta put out the fire, man," he told the dispatcher. "My marijuana plants are burning." When the firefighting team arrived, they found the man sitting in the kitchen with the lights out playing his guitar. He was arrested. Apparently he was arrested both legally and mentally.

911 REPORT

Person answered "no" to the question: "Are you conscious?"

a Man for all Seasons

MAN: Okay, I'm confused. We are in the summertime, or we're still in the wintertime? I'm confused.

DISPATCHER: It's spring.

a Call on the Run

According to an Associated Press article, a forty-five-year-old man led police on a high-speed chase between Oak Ridge, Texas, and Lebanon, Oklahoma. The fleeing felon lost his patience and kept calling 911 asking the operators to tell the police to stop chasing him, but they didn't.

---911 Report---

Eighteen-year-old male couldn't get any rest at home and wanted a ride to the hospital.

Is It Real or Is It Memorex?

DISPATCHER: 911, please state your emergency.

MALE CALLER: Yeah, am I talking to a real operator or is this a recording?

DISPATCHER: This is a real operator, please state your emergency.

MALE CALLER: Are you sure you're a real person—you sort of sound like a recording.

DISPATCHER: [irritated] I'm a real person, sir!

MALE CALLER: Okay. Now you sound like a real operator.

I'm Not the Man I Used to Be

DISPATCHER: 911, what's your emergency?

CALLER: Could you send the police to my house?

DISPATCHER: What's wrong there?

CALLER: I called and someone answered the phone, but I'm not there.

Bagged and Bagged

Two teenagers walked into an AM/PM Mini Mart in San Diego, California, and stuffed their pockets with merchandise. The clerk chased them out of the store and then called 911. Meanwhile, the two senseless shoplifters came back inside and asked the clerk to give them a bag. This gave the police the extra time they needed to apprehend the teenagers as they were leaving the store. I wonder if the clerk asked them, "paper or plastic?"

911 REPORT

"I think my neighbor is a spy."

Unbearable

DISPATCHER: Hello, 911.

WOMAN: Animal Patrol please, hurry, hurry, hurry.

DISPATCHER: Okay, ma'am, what's going on?

WOMAN: It's a black bear—it's squooshed. I mean totally squooshed.

DISPATCHER: What do you mean it's squooshed?

WOMAN: He's flat. Flatter than a flitter.

DISPATCHER: Okay, I'll call Animal Control.

WOMAN: Okay.

DISPATCHER: Okay, bye, bye.

[Later]

DISPATCHER: 911, what's your emergency?

WOMAN: Yeah, this is the lady that just called about the black bear.

DISPATCHER: Yes, ma'am.

WOMAN: It's, it's plastic.

DISPATCHER: It's not a real bear?

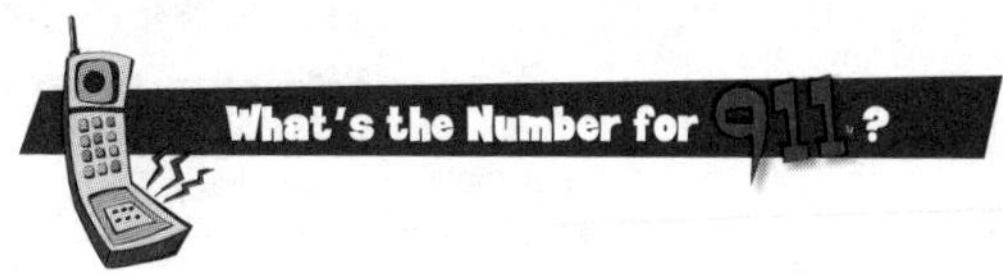

WOMAN: No, but I mean it opened its eyes and said, "Oh!" and that's when I picked up the phone. I didn't even look. And I started giving the stupid thing mouth-to-mouth.

DISPATCHER: Okay, ma'am.

WOMAN: I'm sorry.

DISPATCHER: That's all right. Bye, bye.

You're Only as Old as You Feel

A ninety-year-old man called the Charlotte, North Carolina, emergency center to complain of a consumer fraud. He explained that he recently hired a prostitute but that she left him—dissatisfied. He wanted to file a formal complaint, have the prostitute arrested, and get his money back. When the shocked dispatcher informed him that soliciting a prostitute was a crime, he quickly hung up. Makes you wonder if, because of his age, he was offered a senior citizen's discount.

911 REPORT

"I've been standing all day and my feet hurt."

Who's the Fairest of Them all?

DISPATCHER: 911, what's the nature of your emergency, please?

WOMAN: My son, my son's been shot.

DISPATCHER: Okay, is he breathing?

WOMAN: Yes.

DISPATCHER: All right, then, is he conscious?

WOMAN: Well, I guess so. He's standing up looking at himself in the mirror.

---911 Report---

Police in Aachen, Germany, reported a woman called 911 for assistance because her husband was "refusing to fulfill his sexual obligations."

Beer Nuts

A man in La Vergne, Tennessee, called 911 and requested they send a squad car to his house. The man explained that he had had a fight with his wife and that he needed the police to stop her from pouring out all his beer.

---911 Report---

"Meet complainant regarding a neighbor's rabbit eating complainant's garden."

The 411 on 911

PALM BEACH DISPATCHER: 911 emergency.

CALLER: Hi, I've been getting a lot of calls for someone else and uh, I need to, you . . . I would like a different number and uh . . .

PALM BEACH DISPATCHER: Are you calling 911 because you need your phone number changed?

CALLER: Yes.

PALM BEACH DISPATCHER: Have you called the phone company?

CALLER: I'm not sure how to get in touch with them—but I knew 911.

PALM BEACH DISPATCHER: Look at your phone bill. That's the number you would need to call to get your phone number changed.

CALLER: Oh, could you connect me?

Friction Burns

DISPATCHER: 911. Fire or emergency?

YOUNG BOY: Yeah, there's a fire here. Help, help. Send someone.

DISPATCHER: Just settle down, son. What's your name?

[The caller hangs up. The Charlotte, North Carolina 911 dispatcher locates the address and phone number from the enhanced 911 computer display and calls back the residence. A woman answers the phone.]

DISPATCHER: This is the emergency 911 operator. We received a call that there was a fire at this residence.

WOMAN: [confused] No . . . I don't understand. There's nothing wrong here . . . I don't know why. . . Uh, no, no, sorry, no fire here.

DISPATCHER: We recently received a phone call from a young boy at this number reporting a fire—we were just double-checking.

WOMAN: No, there's no fire here. But as soon as I hang up there's going to be a fire on my son's backside.

That's Some Good Weed

The fire department in Denver, Colorado, responded to an emergency 911 call from the neighboring city of Montbello when a woman reported being trapped in her home. She claimed that hundreds of tumbleweeds—three feet in diameter—had filled her yard and then stacked up against her house, to a height of sixteen feet.

---911 Report---

Young woman called, claiming her baby's temperature was 36.4 degrees and sought assistance in raising it to normal. It was recommended that she look at the Fahrenheit side of the thermometer.

a Great First Date

DISPATCHER: 911, what's your emergency?

MAN: I'm at this woman's house and we're about to have a couple of drinks and suddenly she just drops—just like that, she drops on the floor.

DISPATCHER: All right, sir, just relax.

MAN: She's just laying there. I didn't do nothing, I swear!

DISPATCHER: No one said that you did, sir. Can you tell if she's breathing?

MAN: Gee, I don't know.

DISPATCHER: What's the address?

MAN: The Brookside apartments on Western. She lives at, uh, apartment, oh sh—t, uh, apartment 14D, that's it.

DISPATCHER: Sir, I'm going to tell you how to do CPR, so that you can help her.

MAN: No, I don't think so. I haven't known her that long.

The Writing Is on the Wall

DISPATCHER: 911. Please state your emergency.

CALLER: I'm scared.

DISPATCHER: What's the problem, miss?

CALLER: I just got a Ouija board for my birthday, and now there's writing on my wall and I can't get it off . . . This thing is going back to Kmart first thing in the morning!

a Thin-Skinned Suspect

Silence on the other end of a 911 emergency call is a frightening experience for the dispatchers. It could mean anything: a victim unable to talk, a silent plea for help, or an accidental dialing. So when the Spartanburg Communications/911 Department in South Carolina received an emergency call with no answer, they sent police to investigate. Ironically, when the officers entered the premises, they were quick to find their culprit—a tomato. No, I'm not using Sam Spade vernacular here—it's not a woman—it was a real tomato. Police surmised that the vine-ripened fruit fell from a basket situated above the phone and landed on the preset button for 911. They grilled the tomato for a confession and then let it stew in its own juices. The tomato's lawyer said his client might fry for the offense.

911 REPORT

Man called to advise police that aliens from Los Angeles were tailing residents of Charlotte.

You Should Have Known You Shouldn't Have Called

LONDON DISPATCHER: 999. You've got the go-ahead.

WOMAN: Oh, hello. Um, yeah, I'm just about a bit worried about a friend.

LONDON DISPATCHER: What's—then what's the problem? Why are you calling 999? What's the emergency now?

WOMAN: Um [pause] because I think I'm a bit psychic and I think she might have a car crash tomorrow.

Oh, Pool Boy!

DISPATCHER: 911. Fire or emergency?

CALLER: Fire.

DISPATCHER: Where's the fire, sir?

CALLER: No fire, really.

DISPATCHER: Then what's the problem, sir?

CALLER: No real problem except it's so hot and the pump to our swimming pool is broken.

DISPATCHER: Sir, do you have an emergency?

CALLER: Well, I was hoping that you could send the fire department out to fill our swimming pool.

Chew on This Story

A Washington State man stole a tractor-trailer, sped down the highway, and made a clean getaway. Once his nerves settled down, he realized he was very thirsty. When he noticed a cup in the holder, he took a big swig. Suddenly, he couldn't breathe well and called 911 for help. The operator almost choked after hearing what he drank: The cup was filled with the original driver's tobacco-spit. The thief was arrested, charged with grand theft, taken to jail, and then given a mint.

911 REPORT

Lady got blister from working three days at a Taco Bell.

Scared Straight

DISPATCHER: 911. Fire or emergency?

CALLER: A favor actually. I know you people, the police and all, are busy. But you've got to help me out.

DISPATCHER: I'll do what I can—what's your emergency?

CALLER: I was hoping you could send a policeman over here and have him scare my son into doing his homework.

DISPATCHER: You want us to dispatch a policeman to frighten your son? Is that correct?

CALLER: Yeah, he won't do his homework and I thought if a cop, uh, policeman, showed up and threatened to, like, take him to jail or something, my son might do his homework.

DISPATCHER: I'm sorry, ma'am, we can't do that.

Making a Real Mess of the Situation

Authorities discovered that a sixty-year-old man in Whitehall, Ohio, could have survived a heart attack if his wife had acted faster. It seems the woman refused to call 911 after her husband collapsed: She was afraid the police would arrest her because their house was so messy.

911 REPORT

"I think I've found some stolen property."

Who's the Child and Who's the Adult?

DISPATCHER: 911. How may I help you?

YOUNG BOY: Hello. My mom—we were driving home from a friend's house, and my mom's kind of going delusional and I don't know what to do. She's not taking me home.

DISPATCHER: Your mom did what? What's going on with your mom?

YOUNG BOY: My mom—I think she's delusional. She doesn't know where she's going anymore because I think that she's—we were at a restaurant and she had some drinks, and I don't know if the drinks are affecting her or something.

The Rainbow Confrontation

DISPATCHER: 911, what's the nature of your emergency?

CALLER: You've got to help me out here. Now I'm a good Christian woman and all, but this thing has gone too far.

DISPATCHER: What are you talking about, ma'am?

CALLER: I love the Lord and I love all the people that love the Lord, but you might have to send me a policeman to get him out of my house.

DISPATCHER: Is someone in your house?

CALLER: Yes, and he won't leave.

DISPATCHER: Do you know who he is?

CALLER: I sure do, it's the Reverend Jesse Jackson, and he won't get off my couch.

Comic Stripe

According to the Sheriff's Department in Clyman, Wisconsin, a man called 911 from a local gentlemen's club to report a complaint. The enraged man felt like he had been robbed. He had paid one of the dancers twenty dollars for a lap dance but later he realized that she was not the one who had danced for him.

---911 Report---

A dispatcher working in a Mesa, Arizona, 911 center received a phone call from a man complaining that a power outage was causing him to miss Jay Leno on television.

Frazzled Caller

DISPATCHER: 911. What's your emergency?

FEMALE: Yes, I need the police to come and pick me up, please.

DISPATCHER: Are you in trouble—do you have an emergency?

FEMALE: I just had my hair done.

DISPATCHER: I'm sorry . . .

FEMALE: I need a policeman to come and take me home because it's raining, and I rode my bike to the store. I need them to take me home, or my hair will get wet.

Bumper Bambi

DISPATCHER: 911.

CALLER: I'm reporting a deer on the road. I almost hit it.

DISPATCHER: Is the deer alive?

CALLER: Oh, no, it's run over. Many, many cars. Again and again, and—OH NO!!! NOT AGAIN!

It Wasn't the Hair of the Dog That Bit Them

When two men from Edwardsville, Alabama, who had been drinking, came across a four-foot rattlesnake, they did what anyone would do—they picked it up and started tossing it to one another. The snake did what any snake would do—it bit one of them on the hand and then, when the other man tried to kill it, it bit him on the arm. The two men called 911, but when paramedics arrived, both were semiconscious. One man survived but the other went into cardiac arrest on the way to the hospital and died about an hour after being bitten. We can learn a valuable lesson from these two men: Don't drink and toss snakes!

911 REPORT

"What do I do if a tornado hits?"

What Number Did I Just Call?

DISPATCHER: Allegheny 911.

CALLER: Yeah, hi. I don't really have an emergency, but if I do have one, I was wondering what number to call . . .

An Icy Reception

DISPATCHER: This is Lori, can I help you?

MAN: Yes, I need somebody to get this ice off my windshield. I don't know how to do it, er, I don't have anything to do it with.

DISPATCHER: I'm not sure why you think a police officer's gonna come help you get ice off your windshield.

MAN: I don't have, like, anything to get it off with. And I can't scratch it off.

DISPATCHER: Okay . . . if you don't have an ice scraper you're going to have to use something else with an edge on it that you can get it off with, or start your car and put the defroster on for a while.

MAN: All right, well, can y'all help me or not?

DISPATCHER: Well, I'm helping you by giving you suggestions.

MAN: All right. Later.

See Ya Later . . .

A woman was driving through her neighborhood in Philadelphia, Pennsylvania, with the family pet sitting on her lap—its snout poking out of the driver's side window. When an off-duty police officer saw her drive by, he immediately called 911 to report her. Did he call because the animal wasn't in a car restraint? Nope. He called because the animal was a three-and-a-half-foot alligator. The driver was pulled over, cited for possessing a wild animal within city limits, and, according to a police spokesman the woman, "was very distraught when the alligator (Petey) was taken away from her."

911 REPORT

"I was in a traffic accident yesterday."

What's in That Special Sauce?

DISPATCHER: Sheriff's Department, how can I help you?

WOMAN: Yeah, I'm over here . . . I'm over here at Burger King right here in San Clemente.

DISPATCHER: Uh-huh.

WOMAN: Um, no, not San Clemente. I'm sorry, I live in San Clemente. I'm in Laguna Niguel, I think, that's where I'm at.

DISPATCHER: Uh-huh.

WOMAN: I'm at a drive-through right now.

DISPATCHER: Uh-huh.

WOMAN: I went . . . I ordered my food three times. They're mopping the floor inside, and I understand they're busy. They're not even busy, okay, I've been the only car here. I asked them four different times to make me a Western Barbecue Burger. Okay, they keep giving me a hamburger with lettuce, tomato, and cheese, onions, and I said, "I'm not leaving . . ."

DISPATCHER: Uh-huh.

WOMAN: I want a Western Burger because I just got my kids from tae kwon do. They're hungry, I'm on my way home, and I live in San Clemente.

DISPATCHER: Uh-huh.

WOMAN: Okay . . . she said, she gave me another hamburger; it's wrong. I said four times, I said, "I want it to go." She said, "Can you go out and park in front?" I said, "No, I want my hamburger right." So then the . . . the lady came to the manager. She . . . well whoever she is, she came up and she said, um, she said, um, "Do you want your money back?" And I said, "No, I want my hamburger. My kids are hungry and I have to jump on that toll freeway." I said, "I am not leaving this spot," and I said, "I will call the police," because I want my Western Burger done right! Now is that so hard?

DISPATCHER: Okay, what exactly is it you want us to do for you?

WOMAN: I . . . send an officer down here. I . . . I want them to make me . . .

DISPATCHER: Ma'am, we're not gonna go down there and enforce your Western Barbecue Cheeseburger.

WOMAN: What am I supposed to do?

DISPATCHER: This is . . . this is between you and the manager. We're not gonna go and enforce how to make a hamburger; that's not a criminal issue. There's . . . there's nothing criminal there.

WOMAN: So I just stand here . . . so I just sit here and wait?

DISPATCHER: You . . . you need to calmly and rationally speak to the manager and figure out what to do between you.

WOMAN: She did come up, and I said, "Can I please have my Western Burger?" She . . . she said, "I'm not dealing with it," and she walked away. Because they're mopping the floor, and it's also the fact that they don't want to . . . they don't want to go through there . . . and . . . and . . .

DISPATCHER: Ma'am, then I suggest you get your money back and go somewhere else. This is . . . this is not a criminal issue. We can't go out there and make them make you a cheeseburger the way you want it.

WOMAN: Well . . . that is . . . that . . . you're supposed to be here to protect me.

DISPATCHER: Well, what are we protecting you from, a wrong cheeseburger?

WOMAN: No . . .

DISPATCHER: Is this like . . . is this a harmful cheeseburger or something? I don't understand what you want us to do.

WOMAN: Just come down here. I'm not . . . I'm not leaving.

DISPATCHER: No ma'am, I'm not sending the deputies down there over a cheeseburger. You need to go in there and act like an adult and either get your money back or go home.

WOMAN: She is not acting like an adult herself! I'm sitting here in my car; I just want them to make my kids a . . . a Western Burger.

DISPATCHER: Ma'am, this is what I suggest: I suggest you get your money back from the manager and you go on your way home.

WOMAN: Okay.

DISPATCHER: Okay? Bye-bye.

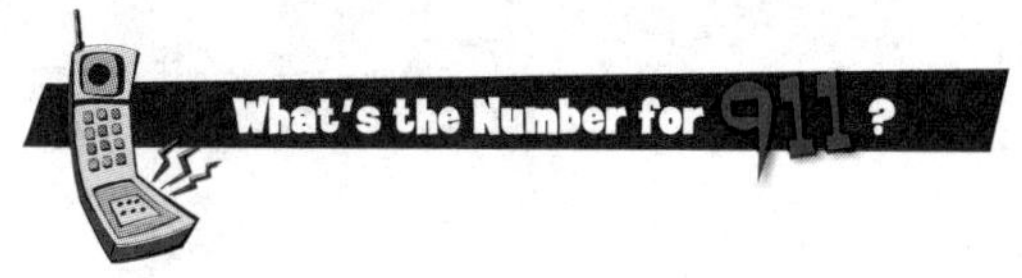

a Snappy Reaction

Police and firefighters in Portland, Oregon, were dispatched to check on a five-year-old boy who had been attacked by an animal. Sometimes this type of call can be quite traumatic: a crying, bleeding child; an animal that has to be hunted down and possibly destroyed; terrified parents. However, when firefighter Hal Westberg arrived on the scene, he realized the situation wasn't that serious. The child had stuck his tongue out at his pet turtle, which in turn chomped down on the boy's tongue and didn't let go. The turtle stayed latched on for fifteen minutes until Westberg slipped his pen in the turtle's mouth and added a little pressure. Then the turtle let go of the child's tongue, and thankfully, the young boy didn't require any medical attention. As for the turtle—he was transferred to a minimum-security tank at a relative's house.

---911 Report---

Complainant, a small boy, called to report that his bird had run out of birdseed.

Hook-Up Hang-up

DISPATCHER: 911, where's your emergency?

WOMAN: It's not an emergency. The only way I know to get in touch with this woman is through Officer Cornet.

DISPATCHER: Okay, I need you to call back on a non-emergency line.

WOMAN: Okay, how do I do that? What's the number?

Chain of Fools

DISPATCHER: 911. Fire or emergency?

MAN: Fire, I guess.

DISPATCHER: How can I help you, sir?

MAN: I was wondering . . . uh, does the fire department put snow chains on their trucks?

DISPATCHER: Yes, sir. Do you have an emergency?

MAN: Well, you know, the snow's been pretty bad here lately.

DISPATCHER: Yes sir, I'm aware of that.

MAN: It's just . . . well, I've spent the last four hours trying to put these darn chains on my tires and I . . . it's just . . . well, do you think once the fire department has their chains on they could come over and help me?

DISPATCHER: Help you what, sir?

MAN: Help me get these damn chains on my car!

911 REPORT

"I want an officer to come out and take care of a low-flying aircraft."

a Criminal Victim

A man from Wichita, Kansas, called 911 to report an armed robbery. He said a man threatened him with a sawed-off shotgun and then stole more than $1,100 in merchandise. When the man informed authorities that, "a pound of marijuana" had been stolen, police were dispatched to his home. The man was later arrested after a drug-sniffing dog located additional marijuana and drug paraphernalia.

---911 Report---

A Uniontown, Ohio, man called 911 to report that someone stole part of the $14,000 he stole from his family.

It's Your Own asphalt

DISPATCHER: 911, what's your emergency?

MAN: Yes, can you tell me what the hell is going on on 55?

DISPATCHER: I'm sorry sir, is there an emergency you wish to report?

MAN: Look, traffic hasn't moved in fifteen minutes. What the hell is the problem?

DISPATCHER: Sir, this is the emergency number . . .

MAN: Yes, yes, yes, I know that—but I'm in a hurry. Is there another way to get to Central from here?

I Can't Take It Anymore!!!

A suspected bank robber was tired of his life on the run and decided to give himself up. The irony was that he called 911 and turned himself in on the same day he robbed the Hospital Trust National Bank in Cranston, Rhode Island. In fact, he was only about a mile away from the bank when he made the call from a pay phone: withdrawn, returned, and taken out of circulation.

---911 Report---

A male caller reported a light in the breezeway of his apartment building has been broken out and wants police to change it.

Runaway Caller

DISPATCHER: 911.

MAN: Yeah, I'm having trouble breathing. I'm all out of breath. Damn . . . I think I'm going to pass out.

DISPATCHER: Sir, where are you calling from?

MAN: I'm at a pay phone. North and Foster. Damn . . .

DISPATCHER: Sir, an ambulance is on the way. Are you an asthmatic?

MAN: No . . .

DISPATCHER: What were you doing before you started having trouble breathing?

MAN: Running from the police . . .

There Was a Crooked Man . . .

DISPATCHER: 911 emergency.

MAN: Yeah, I got's me a problem.

DISPATCHER: What's your problem, sir?

MAN: They's something wrong with my teeth.

DISPATCHER: With your teeth, sir?

MAN: Yeah, my teeth. I got these false teeth here and they don't fit right in my mouth. They're all crooked in my mouth, don't you know.

DISPATCHER: Sir, 911 is for emergencies only.

MAN: I know that and I'm sorry about that. To me, see, this here is an emergency. I need to get my teeth fixed, see. I can't be going to church until someone comes down here and fixes my teeth for me.

He Was Already behind Bars

A 911 hang-up came in from a Tucson, Arizona, residence and, after there was no answer on the callback, police and firefighters were dispatched. When they arrived at the house, they heard what sounded like a woman screaming, but no one opened the door. So, they broke it down, went inside, and stared at the noisy culprit. Oscar, a two-year-old yellow-napped Amazon parrot, ruffled his feathers and squawked at them. His screams "sounded identical to those of a distressed adult female," said one of the officers. The parrot's owners, though, claim the bird did not know how to use the phone. Although the identity of the 911 caller remains a mystery, the bird isn't talking—because he's a parrot, not a stool pigeon.

Plowed Over

DISPATCHER: 911.

CALLER: Yeh, hey. There's a snowplow that's working Biltmore, right?

DISPATCHER: I wouldn't know that, sir.

CALLER: Okay, well, there is. Anyways, how 'bout doing me a favor and getting that guy on the plow to come down my street here and clear the snow.

DISPATCHER: I'm sorry, sir. I can't do that.

CALLER: Come on. I know all about you 911 people—I know you guys got pull. Do me a favor, will ya?

His Arch Enemy

When an off-duty police officer from the University of Texas spotted a foot sticking out of the back of a Dodge minivan, he stopped the vehicle, handcuffed the driver, and called 911 for backup. The foot, however, was made of plastic and was not a dismembered body part.

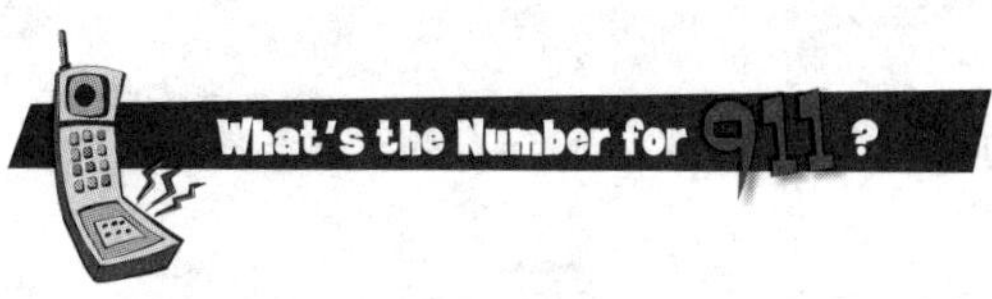

---911 Report---

"Yes, can you tell me the proper time to allow my children to go trick-or-treating?"

Got Milk?

DISPATCHER: 911.

CALLER: I need an ambulance to take me to the hospital.

DISPATCHER: What is the problem, ma'am?

CALLER: My breasts are not lactating.

DISPATCHER: [very dumbfounded] Excuse me . . . ?

CALLER: I gave birth twelve days ago and my breasts are not lactating.

Unclear Reception

DISPATCHER: 911.

MAN: Yeah, my television don't work right.

DISPATCHER: Sir, you've called 911.

MAN: That's right, 'cause the TV in my room—the picture's not too good. Could you send someone to fix it?

DISPATCHER: Sir, are you calling from your home?

MAN: No. I'm in room 32—I'm sharing it with some other fellow. I just want to watch some TV.

DISPATCHER: Sir, you need to call someone at the hospital. 911 is for emergencies only.

MAN: Oh. Could you connect me to the nurses' station?

He's Got a Ticket to Ride

An elderly man from Houston called 911 claiming he had difficulty breathing. When two fire department paramedics arrived at his residence, they found the man sitting on his front porch smoking a cigarette—a packed suitcase on the stoop beside him. He told the stunned paramedics that he had an appointment at the Veterans Administration Hospital, and asked if they could give him a ride, since he had no other way of getting there. The man told them where he wanted to go. I wonder if the paramedics told the man where they would like him to go?

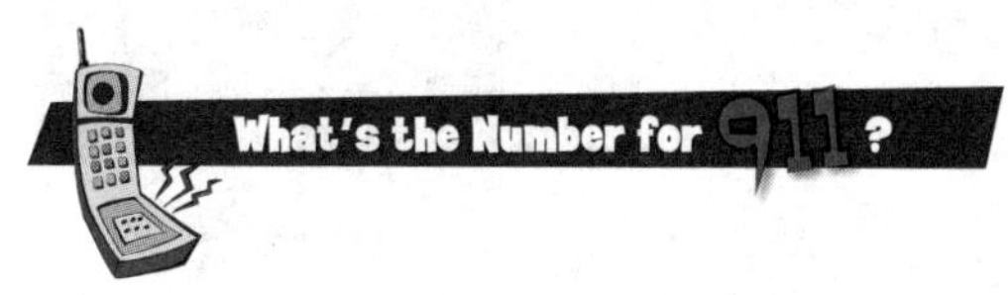

---911 Report---

"Is it okay for a civilian to take a person to the hospital, or does the ambulance have to do it?"

Is Timmy in the Well?

DISPATCHER: 911, this is Jenny, please state your emergency—[pause] 911.

DOG: Woof.

DISPATCHER: Hello?

DOG: Woof.

DISPATCHER: Hello?

DOG: Woof.

DISPATCHER: Can you hear me?

DOG: Woof.

DISPATCHER: If you can hear me we're sending help to you.

DOG: Woof, woof, woof.

Telly Troubles

LONDON DISPATCHER: Police emergency.

BOY: There's a man with an engine on and I can't hear the telly.

LONDON DISPATCHER: Sorry, you called police emergency.

BOY: I did, yes. Is this . . . to stop a man from running an engine opposite my house?

LONDON DISPATCHER: What are you complaining about then?

BOY: I'm complaining that his engine is running and I can't hear the telly!

Breaking in Line

Either the guilt was more than he could bear—or maybe he just had indigestion. When police responded to a 911 hang-up from the Conejo Valley Montessori School in Thousand Oaks, California, they discovered a suspected burglar waiting for them. He was eating a piece of pie, and apparently had also eaten a cupcake. Someone breaking into a school to eat cafeteria food? Now that's a first.

911 REPORT

A six-year-old called 911 because his brother took one of his toys.

Best Little Dispatcher in Texas

DISPATCHER: 911 emergency.

MAN: Yeah, uh, what I would like to do, is, to get the number, um, for a, uh . . . um, uh, a little bit of the house thing, in Reno.

DISPATCHER: I'm sorry.

MAN: Well, uh, it's like a, like a little whorehouse-type deal.

DISPATCHER: This is 911.

MAN: I understand.

DISPATCHER: We're not going to have a number for that.

MAN: You don't have a number?

DISPATCHER: Well, you don't call 911 to get the phone number, sir.

MAN: Okay, thank you.

Rim Shot

DISPATCHER: Fire and ambulance.

CALLER: Yes sir, I need an ambulance for my son—he has his finger stuck in a Hot Wheels car.

DISPATCHER: I'm sorry sir, is this an emergency?

CALLER: Well, it's his favorite one!

Feeling Very, Very Blue

A highly agitated woman called 911 to explain that the old saying "What goes up must come down" wasn't holding true. She told the operator that her boyfriend had taken Viagra after dinner and then they made love for about an hour. But his erection never went down—and it was now seven and a half hours later. The operator realized that it was a hard situation, but it wasn't life threatening, so she gave the woman the best advice she could: "Tell him to take a cold shower."

---911 Report---

Roger's department store called three times asking if they should close during the storm.

An Emergency Drill

AKRON DISPATCHER: What is your emergency?

MAN: I've had a toothache since yesterday. My tooth is all swelled up. I'd like to go to St. Thomas for medication.

AKRON DISPATCHER: Sir, is this an emergency?

MAN: Well, it sure hurts like hell!

Coochi, Coochi, Coo

DISPATCHER: 911.

CALLER: I'm having a baby!

DISPATCHER: All right, stay calm, ma'am.

CALLER: I'm calm, I'm just having a baby! Now!

DISPATCHER: How far apart are the contractions?

CALLER: They seem like they're coming right on top of each other.

DISPATCHER: Has your water broke?

CALLER: Yeah, my water broke about a half hour ago. That's when the contractions started hitting real hard.

DISPATCHER: Can you see if the baby is crowning?

CALLER: What?

DISPATCHER: Look and see if you can see the top of the baby's head.

CALLER: I can't do that.

DISPATCHER: Why not?

CALLER: I still have my clothes on.

DISPATCHER: Ma'am, the paramedics are on their way, so there's no need to worry. I need for you to remove all of your clothing from the waist down so that you can check to see if you're crowning.

CALLER: I ain't gonna do that! I don't want them boys [paramedics] to see my coochie.

911 REPORT

Complainant called about neighbor keeping a pet cow in the yard.

What Is 9 Plus 1 Plus 1?

DISPATCHER: 911.

CHILD: Uh, can you help me with my math homework?

DISPATCHER: Son, you've called the emergency number.

CHILD: Yeah, I know. This is an emergency.

An Itsy Bitsy Phone Call

When a woman saw a low-flying plane dropping "tiny packages with streamers attached," she called a 911 center in Sacramento, California. She was afraid it was a terrorist attack. Since the call came in a few days after the first anniversary of 9/11, police didn't want to take any chances. Deputies investigated and learned of the plane's non-threatening status. It was a student pilot who "happened to work for the public defender's office." However, he claimed he hadn't dropped anything from the plane. So what were the "tiny packages" the woman spoke about? It turned out they were only baby spiders "ballooning" down from the trees.

911 REPORT

"Do you know a good stain remover?"

Clothes Minded

DISPATCHER: 911, what's your emergency?

WOMAN: I heard what sounded like gunshots coming from the brown house on the corner here.

DISPATCHER: Do you have an address?

WOMAN: No, I'm wearing a blouse and slacks. Why?

911 REPORT

"My toilet is plugged. I want you to send someone out to fix it."

a Crushing Problem

DISPATCHER: 911. Fire or emergency?

CALLER: It's an emergency.

DISPATCHER: How can I help you, sir?

CALLER: I'll tell you how you can damn well help me. You can call that g— d— hospital across the street and tell them to shut the hell up.

DISPATCHER: Is there a disturbance at . . . ?

CALLER: The Christ Memorial Hospital—across the damn street here. They're making a racket and I can't g— d— sleep.

DISPATCHER: What's going on there, sir?

CALLER: Just send a policeman over there, or you call them, and tell them to shut off their kidney-stone crusher. That thing has been going all night and I've got to get me some g— d— sleep!

This Is Only a Test

DISPATCHER: York County emergency.

WOMAN: Yes, what is all that racket?

DISPATCHER: Ma'am?

WOMAN: Those sirens—they've been going on for hours, it seems.

DISPATCHER: Those are warning sirens, ma'am. There's high winds that could easily turn into a tornado. We wanted people to be prepared.

WOMAN: Well, that's just fine. But they're hurting my dog's ears and I want you to turn them off.

Dis the Dispatcher

DISPATCHER: Allegheny 911.

CALLER: Oh, I didn't want 911. I wanted the real police.

Smoke 'Em if You Got 'Em

A fifty-seven-year-old man was released on bond providing that he never use the 911 number again—unless it was an actual emergency. It seemed he had called 911 while suffering from a nicotine fit, and asked the dispatcher if they could deliver cigarettes to his home.

---911 Report---

"When does the Burger King open?"
(The caller did not specify which Burger King.)

Not Quite the Lift She Was Expecting

DISPATCHER: 911.

YOUNG BOY: Yeah, excuse me, the babysitter is stuck in the elevator down, uh, the one that brings food down there [i.e., a dumbwaiter].

DISPATCHER: Are you at a house?

YOUNG BOY: Yeah.

DISPATCHER: How old are you?

YOUNG BOY: Seven.

DISPATCHER: You're seven?

YOUNG BOY: Mmm, hum. She went down there accidentally. We put her down there, and when she was down there she was hiding her eyes and we can't get her out 'cause she's too heavy.

DISPATCHER: What was she doing in there?

YOUNG BOY: I told her not to hide in there but . . . we were playing hide-and-seek.

DISPATCHER: Oh, you guys were playing hide-and-seek.

YOUNG BOY: We never, ever, had this thing happen before and I'm not the bad guy. And we also have a German shepherd here.

DISPATCHER: Okay, nobody is going to die though, okay?

YOUNG BOY: No one's going to die, okay.

DISPATCHER: No, she's not going to die, she'll be fine.

YOUNG BOY: All we want is to get her out of there.

DISPATCHER: Yeah, we need to get her out of there. Can you talk to her?

YOUNG BOY: Yes, I can.

DISPATCHER: Tell her that the fire department is coming.

YOUNG BOY: Okay. So stay on the phone until they . . .

DISPATCHER: I'll stay on the phone.

YOUNG BOY: Okay.

When the Bough Breaks

DISPATCHER: 911. Fire or emergency?

CALLER: Now I've called about this before, and you people didn't do anything about it. Now they're back, and I'm getting a little sick and tired of it.

DISPATCHER: What's going on, ma'am?

CALLER: I just think it's the most sickening thing I've ever seen. And I wish you people would do something about it. It's those statue people. They're doing it again. The statue people are having sex in my trees.

Chim Chimery

The *Fort Worth Star-Telegram* reported that when a thirty-five-year-old man and his mother-in-law arrived at her house, the woman realized she had forgotten her keys. She wanted to call a locksmith, but her son-in-law thought his idea was the key to their problem—he would climb down the chimney. "I slid all the way down, but the angle wasn't right, and I worked myself into getting stuck," he said. His mother-in-law finally let her fingers do the walking and she dialed 911. In order to get him out of his grimy, Grinchy situation, firefighters had to demolish the chimney. The man, who later described his actions as "Stuuuuuupid!," advised others: "Listen to your mother-in-law. Don't climb down chimneys. And I probably need to lose weight."

---911 Report---

Female complainant called to say there was a stray cat hanging out in her window well.

Creature Comforts

DISPATCHER: 911.

CALLER: Yes, hello, I'm sorry to bother you. Could you do me a favor, young lady?

DISPATCHER: Yes, ma'am, if I can.

CALLER: Good. You see my kitty, Tex, died a few days ago. Poor little thing—I had to put him to sleep. It was pitiful.

DISPATCHER: I'm sorry to hear that, ma'am.

CALLER: Thank you dear, that's very sweet. But now Tiny is very depressed—just moping around, won't eat—cries all the time.

DISPATCHER: Tiny?

CALLER: Tex's sister.

DISPATCHER: How can I help you?

CALLER: I was wondering if you could send over a policeman to help me console little Tiny. I don't know what to do for the poor thing.

---911 Report---

"Yeah, hi, I was wondering if you could tell me how bad the snow is in Queen City?"

Here's Johnny!

DISPATCHER: 911. Fire or emergency?

WOMAN: [whispering] Help me . . . there's someone in my house.

DISPATCHER: Where are you now, ma'am?

WOMAN: I'm hiding under the bed. Oh, God, someone's coming down the hall. Help . . . quick.

DISPATCHER: Just remain calm and stay on the line.

WOMAN: Hurry, hurry.

DISPATCHER: Officers are on the way, ma'am.

WOMAN: He's trying to get in the door. Please help. Oh, God.

MAN'S VOICE: [muffled] Joan! Joan, are you in there?

WOMAN: Bill? Never mind, it's just my husband.

At Least He Took a Stab at It

A man from Salem, Oregon, made a bizarre attempt to distract a police officer from writing him a speeding ticket. He called 911 and falsely reported a knife stabbing less than a block from his current location, hoping that the officer would be dispatched to investigate the crime—and he would therefore get out of the ticket. But the man wasn't very covert in his attempt. "I just started laughing because I can tell the guy I have in the right front passenger seat is making a fake call," the officer recalled.

911 REPORT

A caller wanted to know how to cook a leg of lamb.

a Real Turkey of a Phone Call

DISPATCHER: 911.

CALLER: Hi, is this the police?

DISPATCHER: This is 911. Do you need police assistance?

CALLER: Well, I was wondering. I don't know who to call. Can you tell me how to cook a turkey? I've never cooked one before.

911 REPORT

(Young Caller) "Hi, I just swallowed a penny. Am I going to die?"

Address Unknown

DISPATCHER: 911. Fire or police?

CALLER: Yeah. Well, police, I guess. Someone stole my mailbox.

DISPATCHER: Can I have your address sir?

CALLER: It's gone.

More Isn't Always Better

According to an article in the *Vancouver Sun*, police in Surrey, British Columbia, responded to a house after a 911 hang-up call and the callback was unresponsive. A sixty-year-old woman told the officers she'd heard that if she dialed 9111 she'd get a recording telling her if the police were tapping the phone. Dialing an extra 1 after 911 is an urban legend and is, of course, false but what is true is that police arrested this woman when they found "a reasonably sized marijuana growing operation" in her house. A sixty-one-year-old man, a fifty-five-year-old man, and a man who had just turned sixty were also arrested but were released later that day. They celebrated their friend's sixtieth birthday together—but they had to settle for blowing out candles—and not blowing some weed.

911 REPORT

"Is this 911?"

Taking a Bite out of Crime

DISPATCHER: 911, what's your emergency?

WOMAN: Someone broke into my house and took a bite out of my ham and cheese sandwich.

DISPATCHER: Excuse me?

WOMAN: I made a ham and cheese sandwich and left it on the kitchen table and when I came back from the bathroom someone had taken a bite out of it.

DISPATCHER: Was anything else taken?

WOMAN: No. But this has happened to me before, you know, and I'm sick and tired of it.

Don't Try This at Home

According to an article in the *Augusta (GA) Chronicle*, a thirty-seven-year-old man died of smoke inhalation after his house caught fire. Although the man escaped the blaze, the smoke overcame him when he went back inside to look for his cell phone—to call 911.

---911 Report---

"I don't have any more credit left on my mobile phone card. What do I do now?"

a Short Fuse

DISPATCHER: 911, where is your emergency?

MAN: I'm sorry, but are the fireworks still on?

DISPATCHER: I'm sorry, you cannot call 911 for that.

MAN: Thank you.

Stop Being So Stubborn

WOMAN: Yeah, we have an emergency out here—there's a girl out here that's giving birth.

DISPATCHER: How far along is she?

WOMAN: Oh, the baby's part-jway out and we can't get it out.

DISPATCHER: Do you know if she was having any complications prior to this?

WOMAN: I didn't even know she was gonna have one.

DISPATCHER: Okay.

WOMAN: And her, the owners are in China. The baby . . . she's walking around, and the baby is not out yet, it's still hangin' there and . . .

DISPATCHER: Okay, I need for her to lie down . . .

WOMAN: I'll let you talk to somebody else.

DISPATCHER: Okay.

MAN: Hello?

DISPATCHER: Okay, is there someone there that knows anything about delivering children?

MAN: Uh, do you understand this is a donkey?

DISPATCHER: Excuse me?

MAN: It's not a person, it's a donkey.

DISPATCHER: Nooooooo . . . that . . . she said there was a lady across the street that was having a baby.

MAN: No, their donkey is having a baby.

DISPATCHER: Okay, let me get hold of Animal Control and I'll get someone out there.

Instant Justice

A twenty-year-old woman from Tucson, Arizona, was angry with the police for arresting her on vandalism charges. She was so mad that she slashed twenty-four tires on six police cars that were parked outside the police station. On the last tire, however, the knife slipped a little, and she cut a huge gash in her hand. "She cut her hand with the butcher knife she used to slash the tires and then called 911," said an unidentified police officer. "This gets even dumber. She told the operator she cut her hand while slashing 'the tires on your [expletive] cars.'" The woman was arrested after being treated at the scene but then released on her own recognizance.

---911 Report---

"Did we just have an earthquake? Where was it centered? How strong was it? What was the damage?"

You Big Baby!

DISPATCHER: 911.

WOMAN: My baby's been shot! My baby's been shot!

Paramedics were dispatched immediately. They reported back that the woman's "baby" was a thirty-one-year-old man.

The One That Got Away

DISPATCHER: Sheriff's Department.

MALE CALLER: Yeah, there's this commercial fishing boat that's been circling Cayucos Pier. It goes up . . . and around . . . and ain't nobody caught nothin' today. I pay an outrageous price to fish in the waters of California, and the fishin's not that great out here as it is—you know what I mean—to have this guy out here, too. I don't want you to do anything. I just wanted you to know.

911 REPORT

"I got a damn Q-Tip stuck in my ear!"

Wishy-Washy

DISPATCHER: 911 emergency.

WOMAN: Yes, is this the police station?

DISPATCHER: Yes, it is. May I help you?

WOMAN: Yeah, okay, I put—this is ridiculous—but I am on Twenty-fourth Street in a car wash stuck inside. I put five dollars in. It put a soak on me, and it won't open the doors, and I'm scared to get out of the car.

DISPATCHER: What's the name of the car wash?

WOMAN: It's uh, I don't know, it's on Twenty-fourth Street. It's right next to a party store or, gosh, I don't even know, I'm just like freaked out.

DISPATCHER: What do you mean, you can't move your car out? Is that what you're saying?

WOMAN: Yeah, the garage doors are shut on both sides and they're not opening.

DISPATCHER: Okay, is there anybody working there or is that one of those self-serves?

WOMAN: It's one of those self-serves. It like put a soak on my car but then it never did anything else—both doors are shut.

DISPATCHER: And you don't know the name of it at all?

WOMAN: It's a super soak or super something—I don't know the name. I'm in a Jeep and you can't even see me inside. I'm freaking out.

DISPATCHER: Is everything running?

WOMAN: No, nothing is running.

DISPATCHER: Why don't you get out? Maybe there's a button on the side of the wall that you can push that will open the doors. There has to be something that you can be able to push.

WOMAN: There's a guy behind me . . . I hope he doesn't start it.

DISPATCHER: Well, if he does then you'd be able to get out.

WOMAN: Yeah, but if he starts the wash I'm going to be super-soaked.

Dumb to the Last Drop

When a woman called 911 in Edmonton, Canada, describing an unusual letter she received in the mail, she caused a full-scale biohazard response from police and firefighters. She explained that after she placed the letter on a table it mysteriously changed from white to pale yellow and then to brown. However, according to the police report, the chameleon letter changed color only because the woman had placed it on top of some spilled coffee. The letter went from Reader's Choice to Taster's Choice.

911 REPORT

"Why is the sun so hot in Arizona?"

a Kick in the Butt

LONDON DISPATCHER: 999 emergency.

WOMAN: [coughing] It's not an emergency, but my husband—I gave him five pounds to get me some cigarettes and cigars and [wheeze] he will not let me have them at all.

LONDON DISPATCHER: Why?

WOMAN: He just won't. He's being crummy. I need them, officer.

Condom-Nation

DISPATCHER: 911.

MAN: [out of breath] Uh, hey, I feel real stupid about this but . . .

DISPATCHER: Sir, do you have an emergency to report?

MAN: You're here to give out information, right?

DISPATCHER: In a way, what's your emergency?

MAN: My girl and I are . . . well, you know. About to do it and . . . sh—t . . . I've got a condom here and . . . Hell, how do you use these things?

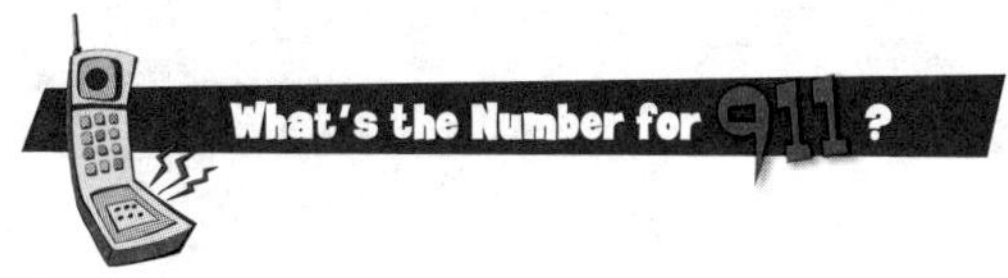

Down in the Mouth

A thirty-four-year-old man from West Valley, Utah, was arrested after calling 911 twelve times in five hours, with most of the calls lasting thirty-minutes, because he had a toothache. He refused an ambulance and didn't want police to come over. However, he did want the phone number of anyone who could help ease his pain. He also wanted illegal drugs off the streets, since he claimed they were given away like trick-or-treat candies—and he wanted it stopped.

911 REPORT

"I can't sleep."

a New Water Bed

DISPATCHER: 911. Fire or emergency?

WOMAN: Yes, I need some help, please.

DISPATCHER: Certainly, ma'am, what's the nature of your emergency?

WOMAN: I need you to send a couple of policemen over to 918 Northwood Drive immediately, please.

DISPATCHER: Can you tell me the problem, ma'am?

WOMAN: Well, I've been sick . . . uh, very sick . . . for about a week now.

DISPATCHER: Yes, ma'am, and what seems to be the problem?

WOMAN: Well, my hot water bottle broke—it just split open and soaked my bed. I would like for you to send a couple of policemen over here and have them flip my mattress. I need to sit down so I'll just leave the door open. Thank you.

DISPATCHER: Hello? Hello?

Don't Leave Home without It

When Dick Muchow from Phoenix, Arizona, broke his ankle, his friend, Doug Steakley, grabbed a cell phone from Muchow's backpack and called 911. So why is this story in a book about weird 911 calls? At the time, the two men were 12,700 feet up on Lizard Head Peak in Colorado. Strangely enough, since there was little to block the phone's signal, several 911 centers received the call and a team of rescuers was sent by helicopter to save the hurt mountaineer and his friend. I hope the two mountaineers didn't bring a cell phone on their hike so they could order a pizza.

911 REPORT

"Is it a burn day?"

This Caller Is Nuts

DISPATCHER: 911, what's the problem?

WOMAN: I have a large tree in my backyard . . . there's a squirrel stuck in the tree.

DISPATCHER: Ma'am, this is a squirrel? In a tree? What's the problem?

WOMAN: It's been there for about an hour. It's crying; it needs help. There's a problem.

DISPATCHER: Ma'am, sorry, but this isn't necessarily a police issue. It's a wild animal, sitting in a tree. It's supposed to be doing that. The squirrel will be okay. It'll climb down when it's ready.

WOMAN: Are you telling me you're not sending me an officer?

DISPATCHER: Sorry ma'am, this isn't a police issue. An officer wouldn't be able to do anything. The squirrel will be just fine, really.

WOMAN: But police officers help people in need, right?

DISPATCHER: Yes, ma'am. Squirrels are not people.

WOMAN: Well, never mind, anyway. You've spent so much time explaining why an officer won't help me, the squirrel left. Thanks.

Striking the Wrong Cord

Fourteen-year-old Stephanie was singing Christmas carols in her Cloverdale, British Columbia, home when a neighbor called 911 to report a woman screaming. The girl's mother met police at the door and explained that no one was screaming, it was simply Stephanie singing. "I know my voice is bad and I'm just assuming she has my genes," she said. Officers reported that the young girl was "exercising her vocal cords" and there was no "danger—except perhaps to surrounding windows."

911 REPORT

"My dog is stuck under the house."

Cat and Mouse

DISPATCHER: 911.

CALLER: Yes, well, I called the vets and they were no help. I was hoping you could.

DISPATCHER: If I can. What's your emergency?

CALLER: My cat, Terrance, caught a mouse. I got the little mouse away before Terrance could kill it. But the silly old cat broke that little mouse's leg.

DISPATCHER: Ma'am?

CALLER: Do you know where I could go to get a cast put on that poor little thing's leg? I'll take care of it until it gets better, don't you worry about that.

Local Yokel

DISPATCHER: 911. What is your emergency?

FEMALE CALLER: Yes, I'm at a pay phone, and I can't get through on a local call.

DISPATCHER: Ma'am, you have reached 911.

FEMALE CALLER: Uh hum. Well . . . I can't make my call.

DISPATCHER: Ma'am, you have dialed 911. 911 is for emergencies only.

FEMALE CALLER: Uh hum. So . . . well, I still can't make my call.

911 REPORT

"There is a loud party next door."

---911 Report---

Mount Olivet Road NE, 1200 block, March 30. An Animal Control officer responding to a call about a snake in a bathroom reported that the snake was actually a hair band.

Leaf Me Alone

DISPATCHER: 911?

MAN: Yeah, my neighbors are committing a crime on my property.

DISPATCHER: Sir?

MAN: They're polluting my pool. They're allowing the leaves from their trees to float over the fence and land in my pool.

DISPATCHER: Sir, have you tried speaking to your neighbors about this?

MAN: No. That's not my job—that's your job!

Lockdown

DISPATCHER: Central Metro 911, what's the address of the emergency?

WOMAN: I'm locked in my car, my battery's shut down . . .

DISPATCHER: You're locked in your car?

WOMAN: Yes, I can't . . . my power's shut down on my car . . .

DISPATCHER: Uh, huh.

WOMAN: And I'm starting to hyperventilate. I'm starting to freak out.

DISPATCHER: Now, ma'am, you think your battery died?

WOMAN: Yes.

DISPATCHER: So, okay, and you tried the handle, right? It won't let you out that way?

WOMAN: No, ma'am, it won't let me do anything, and I'm—

DISPATCHER: Can you, did you, can you actually see the top of your lock? You know, on the door, can you see what it's . . .

WOMAN: No, it's . . . Oh, my gosh.

DISPATCHER: Yeah, just pull it up, baby.

[*click*]

WOMAN: Okay, I'm embarrassed.

DISPATCHER: You can get out now, right?

WOMAN: I'm out. Thank you. I am so embarrassed.

DISPATCHER: That's okay. All right.

Worse Than the Bundy Family

An ambulance crew was dispatched to a Toronto home after a 911 call about a domestic dispute with injuries. When paramedics arrived they treated the twenty-three-year-old man for a broken arm and shoulder and various other wounds. His wife suffered from knife wounds to her chest, back, and legs, and was also treated at the scene.

Apparently, the couple, who were watching *Married with Children,* began arguing over who was prettier—Katey Sagal, who plays Peg Bundy or Christina Applegate, who plays her daughter, Kelly. When the argument escalated, the wife slashed her husband in the groin with a wine bottle. Things calmed down for a while; the wife treated her husband's wounds, and they sat down to watch the show again. Minutes later, however, the argument flared once more. The husband stabbed his wife in the chest, back, and legs and, during the scuffle, suffered a broken arm and shoulder. Al Bundy would have been proud.

---911 Report---

"I've got a palmetto bug that I can't get out of my house."

Eat and Get Gas!

DISPATCHER: Sheriff's Department.

MAN: Yeah, I just ate at [fast food restaurant] and I've been puking my guts out for forty-five minutes. You know, I'm really sick. And I was wondering, did you get any calls from anyone else about anybody gettin' sick from there?

DISPATCHER: No sir, we haven't.

MAN: Okay, well, I was just wondering.

Only the Lonely

DISPATCHER: Sheriff's Department.

WOMAN: Hi, I just got home from a trip and, this is really embarrassing, but somebody left one of those blow-up dolls in my yard. I mean, I can't pick it up and put it in the trash. What are the neighbors going to think when they see me carrying this thing across my yard?

DISPATCHER: Couldn't you just let the air out?

911 REPORT

"Is the road over Tehachapi Pass open?"

His Own Cross to Bear

A twenty-three-year-old man from Somerset County, Vermont, had a passion to commit suicide, so he built a cross in his living room and attempted to crucify himself by nailing one of his hands to the crossbeam with a fourteen-penny nail. But he quickly discovered that his calvary attempt needed the help of the cavalry. "When he realized that he was unable to nail his other hand to the board, he called 911," said Sheriff Barry DeLong. According to the *Bangor Daily News*, DeLong reported that it wasn't clear if the man called to be pried off the cross or if he wanted help nailing down his free hand.

---911 Report---

Female called to complain that cars are parked in the street.

Man of the Year Award

DISPATCHER: What's your emergency?

CALLER: Can you tell me what happened to my girlfriend?

DISPATCHER: I will try.

CALLER: Well, we were having sex. We really started going at it, and she started breathing hard and then passed out at the end. I thought she wasn't breathing so I started doing CPR on her. She came to. She is sleeping now and I think she is fine but I just wanted to know—what happened to her?

DISPATCHER: Sir, I think it was just YOU—if you want I can send a medic truck over to see if she is okay.

CALLER: Oh no, she is sleeping now. I think she should be all right in the morning.

Full of Hot Air

DISPATCHER: 911, what's the nature of your emergency?

WOMAN: Yes, 911. My cat has floated up to the ceiling and I can't get her down.

DISPATCHER: Excuse me, ma'am. Did you say floated?

WOMAN: Yes. It's the strangest thing. I know you're going to think I'm crazy.

DISPATCHER: No, ma'am.

WOMAN: It's just . . . well, she won't come down and I don't know how she got up there in the first place.

DISPATCHER: Is the cat on a shelf or something?

WOMAN: No, she's just floating in the air—it's a little scary. Could you please send someone out to help me?

DISPATCHER: I can give you the number for the police, 911 is for emergencies only . . . I'm sorry.

WOMAN: Well, I can't find my glasses. I'm afraid I can't see the numbers of the phone too well—could you dial it for me?

Police were dispatched to the woman's residence. It turned out the mysterious "floating" cat was actually a helium balloon. The woman's daughter and grandson had visited her earlier that evening and the young boy accidentally left the balloon behind. Police found the woman's glasses and discovered that her real cat was sleeping soundly on her bed.

Once Bitten . . .

DISPATCHER: 911, what's the nature of your emergency?

WOMAN: Yeah, I've been bit by a snake.

DISPATCHER: Did you say a snake, ma'am?

WOMAN: Yeah, a snake. It bit me on the leg. Is it poisonous?

DISPATCHER: I don't know, ma'am.

WOMAN: Look, a damn snake bit my leg and all I want to know is, is it poisonous?

DISPATCHER: Ma'am, everything is going to be all right. An ambulance will be there in moments. Are you feeling dizzy or nauseous?

WOMAN: No, I feel fine. I just want to know if that snake was poisonous. A brown snake, okay. A brown snake with, like, stripes or something—you got it. A brown, striped snake. Now can you tell me if it's poisonous!!!

DISPATCHER: Paramedics will be able to tell you if the snake was poisonous or not.

WOMAN: Well, that's just great. But I'd sort of like to know now, if you don't mind!

An ambulance arrived a short while later and the woman was safely taken to the hospital—the snake was not poisonous.

The Joker's Wild

A woman from Medina, Ohio, was shocked to see her eighteen-year-old son offering to bring in the groceries from the car. "Call 911. I'm having a heart attack," she said in jest. He did, but after he realized his mother was being sarcastic, he redialed 911 to cancel the emergency—but it was too late. "I thought he knew I was joking," the woman said when the police arrived. "He knows I have been a little stressed lately," she added. Then she explained that she was only joking because her son usually had to be forced into doing chores around the house. "It figures. The first time he actually does something I ask, and it's wrong," she joked. I'll bet she never asks him to do anything else—maybe that was his plan all along.

911 REPORT

"I was wrestling and I think I pulled my thumb out of its socket."

Watch This Caller Closely

DISPATCHER: Smith County 911, what's your emergency?

WOMAN: Uhh, I'm watching a movie and the guy's beating another guy with a bat.

DISPATCHER: A movie?

WOMAN: Got it from Blockbuster.

DISPATCHER: Okay, and what do you want me to do about that? What are you wanting?

WOMAN: I don't . . . what can you do?

DISPATCHER: There's nothing we can do. If you don't want to watch the movie, then turn it off.

WOMAN: All right. Thank you. Bye.

---911 Report---

Calle Juanita, 26000 block: Deputies responded to a 911 hang-up call to learn the resident's daughter had recently learned how to call 911 in school and thought she would give it a try, 3:25 p.m., March 17.

—Dana Point, California, news section of the *Orange County Register*

---911 Report---

Man requesting police to investigate the owl that was sitting on a telephone pole.

Wait a Spell

DISPATCHER: 911. Fire or emergency?

MAN: Yeah, I heard some gunshots across the street and need someone to come see what's happened.

DISPATCHER: Is anyone hurt?

MAN: How the hell should I know? Like I said, I heard gunshots and now you guys need to come down here and find out what the hell is going on.

DISPATCHER: What's your address?

MAN: 1402 West Palimar.

DISPATCHER: And could I have your name, please?

MAN: All right. It's Frank Wymarian.

DISPATCHER: Sir, could you please spell your name?

MAN: [irate] That's "W" as in Williams and "Y" as in why.

Circling the U

A man entered a U-Gas Mini Mart in High Ridge, Missouri, near St. Louis with the intention of robbing the convenience store. However, when he demanded money, the clerk simply refused. This stunned the would-be robber so much that he left the store in a huff and went back to his car. The clerk called 911, and then followed the man outside to write down his license plate. The robber was really annoyed now and he chased the clerk back into the store and then began driving his car around in circles and screeching his tires. Deputies arrived at the convenience store to find the cruising criminal still circling the parking lot.

911 REPORT

"I need someone to take my dog to the vet."

Up the Down Staircase

DISPATCHER: 911. Fire or emergency?

CALLER: It's my girlfriend. She's hurt pretty bad.

DISPATCHER: Where is she hurt, sir?

CALLER: Well, I was having a drink, minding my own business, and she started an argument with me. Next thing I know her ass is falling down the stairs. She hasn't moved, so I thought I'd call you guys.

DISPATCHER: Did she just fall?

CALLER: No, she just didn't fall . . . I helped her!

911 REPORT

"I'm a senior citizen and I need someone to shovel my walk, please."

Judge Not, Least Ye Be Judged

The court clerk's eyes widened in shock when she read the note a Denver judge gave her: "Blind on the right side. May be falling. Please call someone." The clerk fearing for the judge's health, called 911, and requested help immediately. When the clerk told the judge that paramedics were on their way, the judge looked horrified. She then pointed to the drooping venetian blinds on the right side of the courtroom. When the paramedics arrived, the judge interrupted a drunk driving case she was presiding over and informed them that she was fine and thanked the emergency team for their prompt response. I just hope she makes her judgment calls a little clearer than her notes.

911 REPORT

"Could someone stop by my house and take me grocery shopping?"

Out of Order

DISPATCHER: 911. What's your emergency?

WOMAN: I need assistance at Jim's on Lincoln and Woodbury.

DISPATCHER: I know, what's the problem?

WOMAN: They stole my damn dollar . . . he won't fix my taco—I ain't havin' no rice in it . . . He's holdin' my dollar and ten cents!

DISPATCHER: Hold on, hold it, slow down. What's going on? Hello?

WOMAN: What did I say?

DISPATCHER: I, I can't tell. You're yelling at me now.

WOMAN: I need assistance. I want my dollar or my taco.

DISPATCHER: You're having a problem with a taco?

WOMAN: The order, bitch! Pardon me.

DISPATCHER: Excuse me?

WOMAN: I am upset.

DISPATCHER: I know and you have to calm down and tell me what's going on here, now.

WOMAN: You bring your ass and get my *&^@&! taco up in here!

DISPATCHER: My, my ass is staying in the, in the office here, so . . .

WOMAN: You're not coming?

DISPATCHER: . . .You need to—you need to—

WOMAN: You ain't givin' no assistance to me?

DISPATCHER: You need to calm down and tell me something here. Okay?

WOMAN: All right, bitch, just . . .

DISPATCHER: Wha, why are you calling me names?

WOMAN: Look, are you comin' or not?

DISPATCHER: As far as I'm concerned . . .

WOMAN: I want my dollar!

DISPATCHER: . . . You can have that taco.

WOMAN: I want my damned dollar! What?

DISPATCHER: I said, as far as I'm concerned, you can have the taco.

WOMAN: I want my dollar or my taco!

airhead—air Gun

DISPATCHER: 911.

MAN: I don't have an emergency, but I have a quick, very quick, question. I would like to know if it's okay to shoot my BB gun inside my house.

DISPATCHER: Sir, I can't have you on this line.

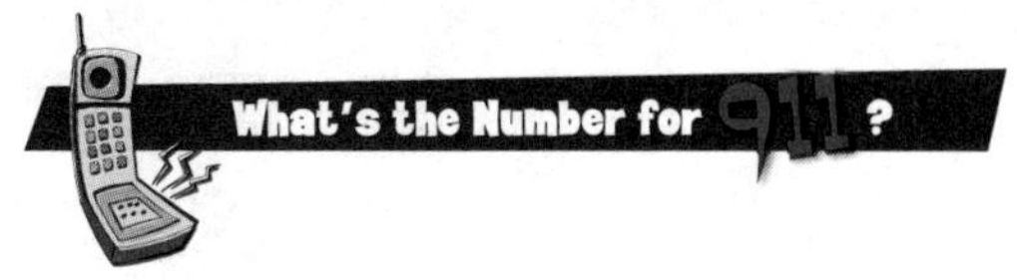

Party On!

DISPATCHER: 911, please state your emergency.

CALLER: Yeah, okay, Bill got hurt.

DISPATCHER: All right, who is Bill?

CALLER: Just some dude I know. We were tossing the Nerf around and the TV fell and cut up his leg . . . like.

DISPATCHER: We'll send someone right over.

CALLER: Get the keg outta here, dude!

Crap Out of Luck

After New York City dispatchers received a call about a man in trouble, they knew this guy was going to raise a real stink. Paramedics arrived and treated Tim Young of Brooklyn for asphyxiation after he accidentally fell into a filled sewage vat. The man was held under the surface for three minutes before co-workers finally heard him pounding on the tank. "It's kind of embarrassing when you think about it," said Young. "I mean, here I am passing out under all that mess and I'm thinking to myself: Hey, do I really want to be rescued? If they rescue me, I'll have to explain how I fell in. As it turns out, I guess I did want to be rescued bad enough." When reporters asked Young how he happened to fall into the tank, he refused to comment.

911 REPORT

"My phone doesn't work."

I'll Tell You Where to Go!

DISPATCHER: Allegheny 911.

CALLER: I'm lost. Can you give me directions?

The Man Who Cried, "Eureka!"

A man from Portland, Oregon, was taken to an emergency clinic after a 911 call for help. The man was suffering from severe bruising and lacerations on his penis and testicles. The cause? A handheld vacuum cleaner. The excuse? He claimed to have been vacuuming wearing only a bathrobe and then tripped as his robe fell open. "It always does that," he said. It was when he fell on the still-whirring vacuum cleaner that his privates got caught up in the beater bar. The man required fifteen stitches and an overnight stay at the clinic. As to what he'll do in the future about his errant robe: "I keep meaning to rig up some kind of tie for it, but I never do. I guess I'll get around to it now." Boy, don't you just hate it when that happens?

911 REPORT

"Someone needs to get out here and shovel my walk!"

Miss-Conception

DISPATCHER: 911, what's the nature of your emergency?

MAN: My wife is pregnant and her contractions are only two minutes apart!

DISPATCHER: Is this her first child?

MAN: No, you idiot! This is her husband!

911 REPORT

"Do you have some time to just talk?"

Saddle Up

DISPATCHER: 911. Fire or emergency?

CALLER: This is just the most ridiculous thing. I want the police down here now.

DISPATCHER: What's the problem, sir?

CALLER: I'm a taxpayer and I want the police down here to get rid of these hoodlums that have been coming on my property.

DISPATCHER: Do you have an emergency, sir?

CALLER: Damn straight I do. These three boys jumped my fence . . . I'm watching all this from the upstairs window . . . and, pretty as you please, jump on the back of my sheep and start riding them around my property.

DISPATCHER: They're riding your sheep?

CALLER: Like a damn horse!

Run, Run, as Fast as You Can . . .

"Mom, it's the firemen. I told them we have an emergency," said a four-year-old Bazetta, Ohio, boy, during his phone call to 911. Then he added, "and we really do." It was just two weeks before Christmas, and the police who were dispatched to the scene discovered the burning emergency was—the boy's mother had overbaked the gingerbread man. An officer on the scene talked to the boy about the importance of the emergency number. "He told the boy that because the gingerbread man doesn't breathe and doesn't bleed, there was no need to call 911," Police Chief Robert Jacola said. The scorched gingerbread man and five other cookie "burn victims" were taken to the 911 Center. "We just want to keep them for sentimental value," said dispatcher Roger Laird.

---911 Report---

"Give me the number for the police. And don't give me any crap about looking up the number myself—I don't have time."

Ironing Out Their Differences

DISPATCHER: 911, what's your emergency?

MAN: Yeah, I'm hurt. My wife hit me with a smooth.

DISPATCHER: A what, sir?

MAN: A smooth.

DISPATCHER: I, uh . . .

MAN: You know, the thing you use to smooth out your clothes with. It's uh . . .

DISPATCHER: Iron?

MAN: I don't know what it was made out of but it hurt like hell.

Millie Helper's Revenge

DISPATCHER: Allegheny 911.

WOMAN: I would like to be connected with a police officer.

DISPATCHER: Okay, what do you need?

WOMAN: It's really not an emergency . . . maybe I can go down to the station.

DISPATCHER: It's okay that you called, ma'am. How can we help you?

WOMAN: It's really nothing, but there is a fire in my kitchen and I'd like to speak with an officer about this. But can you tell them if they want to come here, please don't use any lights or sirens. That's very embarrassing, and my neighbors are very nosy.

Going Off Half Cocked

A cocky twenty-one-year-old man shoved his .22 caliber pistol into the waistband of his pants. (He was feeling less cocky, however, when the gun fired and shot him in the groin.) He then managed to hobble to his girlfriend's apartment in Pasadena, Maryland, and called 911. A friend, who was also at the apartment, picked up the gun and stuck it in *his* back pocket. Unfortunately, the gun went off again and left a new hole in the friend's butt. The police arrived and were able to confiscate the gun without shooting themselves.

---911 Report---

"Yeah, I need one of you guys to come out here and help me push my car out of the snow."

Second Time's a Charm

Paramedics rushed to the Kentucky home of thirty-two-year-old Phillip Johnson after he called about a gunshot wound. When they arrived, Johnson told them that he had purposely shot himself above his left nipple because he wanted to see what it would feel like. The paramedic's report stated that Johnson was "screaming about the pain," over and over. However, a year later, Johnson called 911 after he shot himself again with his .22-caliber rifle. He confessed that the first shooting "felt so good" that he had to do it again. Well, at least the guy's got a hobby.

911 REPORT

(Very young caller) "Do you know Santa Claus' phone number?"

a Real Nanny 911 Call

DISPATCHER: 911, what's the address of your emergency?

WOMAN: Um, 15____ Shawhill Road.

DISPATCHER: 15___ Shawhill?

WOMAN: Yeah.

DISPATCHER: What's going on there?

WOMAN: I need a nanny.

DISPATCHER: A nanny?

WOMAN: Yep, this is a nanny 911. I need a babysitter and some friends and [sigh] yeah.

DISPATCHER: Okay, ma'am, I'm not understanding what you need. [pause] What's going on?

WOMAN: I just need a babysitter.

DISPATCHER: Okay, 911 does not provide a babysitter, ma'am.

WOMAN: Okay, thank you.

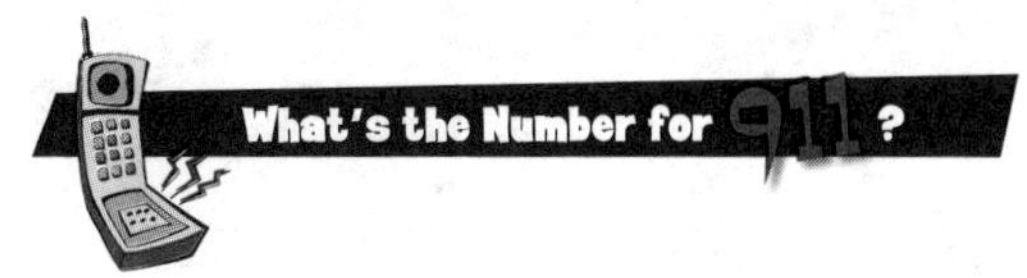

Ring around the Drain

DISPATCHER: 911, what's your emergency?

WOMAN: I dropped my engagement ring in the toilet and I don't trust plumbers. Can you please send a policeman to get it out?

The Venus Fly Sofa

Neighbors in Scottsdale, Arizona, called 911 when they heard frightened but muffled screams coming from the house next door. Rescue workers arrived promptly, and discovered that a woman was trapped in her sleeper sofa. She claimed the sofa just snapped shut on her. It took paramedics four hours to remove the woman from her own sofa. I've heard of a coach potato before—but this woman almost grew roots.

911 REPORT

"We might [cough] need the fire department here [cough]."

Wake Up and Smell the Coffee

DISPATCHER: 911. Fire or emergency?

MAN: Yeah, uh, I'm on a business trip and I know you guys are up early anyway, so . . .

DISPATCHER: Sir, do you have an emergency?

MAN: Well, like I was saying, since you guys are up early in the morning anyway—I was wondering if you could give me a wake-up call.

DISPATCHER: Excuse me, sir?

MAN: A wake-up call. I'm at the Rockford Hotel in room 312. The number is . . .

DISPATCHER: I'm sorry, sir. I can't help you unless there is an emergency in progress.

MAN: Oh. Well. I just thought, you know, you're already awake . . . what's the big deal!

[The caller hangs up]